DON'T JUST SIT THERE

For Ages 6-8

Bible Stories That Move You

Also available from Abingdon Press:

Don't Just Sit There
Bible Stories That Move You
For Ages 3-5

Editor: LeeDell Stickler
Production Editor: Cindy Martin
Designer: Paige Easter
Cover Photo: Ron Benedict

Illustrators: pages 10, 12-15, 19, 25-26, 29, 33, 47-48, 54, 92, 94-95, 97, 101, 106-107 by Jim Padgett; pages 11, 22, 39, 40, 42, 58-59, 61, 63-64, 78-79, 81-82, 87, 104, 108 by John Ham; pages 52, 60, 71, 73, 99 by Charles Jakubowski; Pages 28, 67, 84 by Barbara Upchurch; pages 86, 91 by Robert S. Jones; pages 57, 62, 77 by Brenda Gilliam; pages 72, 80 by Tom Dunnington/John Walter and Associates; page 20, Sandy C. Bauer; page 53, Pat Bridges.

DON'T JUST SIT THERE

Bible Stories That Move You

Abingdon Press
Nashville

DON'T JUST SIT THERE
BIBLE STORIES THAT MOVE YOU
FOR AGES 6-8

Copyright © 1997 by Abingdon Press

ISBN 0-687-122007

Catologing-in-Publication Data has been requested from Library of Congress

Unless otherwise noted, Scripture quotations are from the New Revised Standard Version Bible.
Copyright 1989 by the Division of Christian Education
of the National Council of the Churches of Christ in the USA.
Used by permission.

97 98 99 00 01 02 03 04 05 06 —10 9 8 7 6 5 4 3 2 1

MANUFACTURED IN THE UNITED STATES OF AMERICA

Table of Contents

Advent and Christmas

Followers of Jesus

Parables and Teachings of Jesus

Lent and Easter

Pentecost and the Early Church

Paul and His Friends

The Bible, Sunday School, and Other Things

Storytelling

As a five-year old, I attended kinder garten at the First United Methodist Church in our town. My most vivid memory is Mrs. Knight sitting on the floor holding a huge black book to read us a Bible story. She seemed to live the story as she read, her eyes dancing with excitement or her face frowning with sadness.

Storytelling is an important part of teaching children. Below are some keys to good storytelling. Use these ideas to unlock the door to a Bible experience your children will long remember!

1. **Prepare for story time.**
   Read and study the story several times, until you know the plot and characters.
2. **Feel the story.**
   Don't hesitate to ad-lib. Add or take out words as you feel the need. Tell the story with your personal tough, using the author's words as a base. Understand the feelings and conversation of the different characters.
3. **Prepare your space.**
   Have story time in a comfortable, cozy area of the room. Sit in a low chair or on the floor with the children surrounding you. Sit away from other noisy activities. Children need to be able to see and touch the pictures, so allow plenty of room for closeness. Children do better in a small group.
4. **Vary your voice.**
   Change the inflection and speed of your voice as the plot changes. Speak quickly and loudly for excitement; slowly and quietly for suspense; and use pauses for emphasis or expectation.
5. **Utilize good props.**
   Try using a flannelboard or a puppet to help make the story more interesting. If the plot includes nature items, have these available;

if food, have some to taste.
6. **Practice telling the story.**
   Tell the story to your friends or coworkers. If you have young children, tell it to them. Practice in front of a mirror.
7. **Look at the children.**
   As you read or tell the story, eye contact with the children makes the story come alive! You can tell how children are responding!
8. **Be sensitive to the audience.**
   Listen to the children's comments and questions. React to them, but avoid preaching or moralizing. Observe their facial expressions or any vocal responses such as "ooh."
9. **Be creative.**
   Use background mood music or dress in a costume to create a mood or interest in the story.
10. **Evaluate.**
    How did the children react to the story? How could you improve your telling of the story?

How to Choose a Story
—Is it appropriate for the age level (vocabulary, length of sentences, visual imagery?"
—Does it include experiences familiar to the child?
—Does the story involve movement and action?
—Is there appropriate and interesting conversation?
—Are there areas of suspense, leading to a conclusion?
—Does the story build to an exciting climax?
—Is it picturesque? Can the child see images and pictures?
—Does it challenge the child in some way that helps the child be a better person?

Don't Just Sit There!

by Daphna Flegal and
LeeDell Stickler

Don't just sit there!
Let them move and shout.
Don't just sit there!
Let them hop about.

'Cause children can learn
As they wiggle and wave.
'Cause children can learn
In many, many ways.

Creation

Experiencing God's World Through the Senses

by Daphna Flegal

As you read the following poem, the children will contribute things that they like to see, hear, taste, touch, and smell in God's world at the appropriate place in the poem.

Say: God gifted each of us with many ways to experience God's world. We can experience it through sight, sound, taste, touch, and smell.

Bright blue skies and fluffy clouds,
Soft green grass and pink seashells,
I like what I see in God's world.
What do you like to see? (*Teacher may point to one or more children at this point.*)
(*Repeat things the children name.*)
It is good. It is good. It is very very good!

Singing birds and chirping bugs,
Quacking ducks and laughing friends,
I like what I hear in God's world. (*Teacher may point to one or more children at this point.*)
What do you like to hear?
(*Repeat things the children name.*)
It is good. It is good. It is very very good!

Purple grapes and yellow squash,
Apple juice and small green peas,
I like what I taste in God's world.
What do you like to taste? (*Teacher may point to one or more children at this point.*)
(*Repeat things the children name.*)
It is good. It is good. It is very very good!

Cold snowflakes and kittens' fur,
Squishy mud and Grandma's hug,
I like what I touch in God's world.
What do you like to touch? (*Teacher may point to one or more children at this point.*)
(*Repeat things the children name.*)
It is good. It is good. It is very very good!

Popping corn and one red rose,
Tall pine trees and fresh damp earth,
I like what I smell in God's world.
What do you like to smell? (*Teacher may point to one or more children at this point.*)
(*Repeat things the children name.*)
It is good. It is good. It is very very good!

Directions:
Continue the message by providing these experiences for the children to see, hear, taste, touch, smell.

Sight (*a glittery rock, a plant, a flower, candle*)
Sound (*bell, potato chips, musical instrument*)
Taste (*pickle, chocolate candy, honey in a dish*)
Smell (*garlic, cinnamon, perfume, coffee grounds, lemon*)
Touch (*silk scarf, plush animal, sandpaper, cotton balls, feather, ice cube*)

Based on Genesis 1:1-2:4

It Was Good
by LeeDell Stickler

Teach the children the signs for the response.
Let them practice several times before beginning.

It

Was

Very

Good

In the beginning,
there was nothing but nothing.
Nothing but nothing,
nothing but nothing.
Then God made a something
from all of this nothing.
God made us a world.
And it was good.

And this world that was nothing
appeared very dark.
So, God took the darkness
and God took the light,
And God made the day
and God made the night.
And it was good.

Now, this world that was nothing
was not very neat,
So, God took the land
and God took the sea
And out of the nothing,
gave them places to be.
So, God took the sky
and set it in place
Over the land and the sea
in just the right space.
And it was good.

Now that nothing began
to look almost like something,
But still all in all
there wasn't much there.
So, God put some green growing
things on that nothing
And placed them on all
of the spots that were bare.
Green growing things
now filled every space,
Green growing things grew
in every last place
And it was good.

Then God put a sun
in the sky of that something,
A bright yellow sun
that shone down on the land.
And God put a moon
in the sky of that something
A pale, silver moon
that shone down on the sand.
And God filled the sky up
with jillions of stars
And planets named Venus
and Neptune and Mars.
And it was good.

That nothing now looked
a great deal more like something
But it still wasn't finished
according to plan.
There was nothing below
that was moving about,
Nothing below that could swim
or could shout.
So, God made some somethings,
some great feathered somethings
That flew in the air
with their great feathered wings
And God made some scaly-like
things for the seas
And furry-skinned beasts
that could live in the trees.
And God filled that something
that used to be nothing
With creatures of fur and of scales
and of wings.
And it was good.

That nothing but nothing
indeed was now something
But still incomplete
in the great plan of things.
"I need something special,
something loving and caring,
Some unselfish creature

that doesn't mind sharing."
So, God did some thinking
and this was the plan.
God made some people—
a woman and a man.
"They'll care for my green things,
My great feathered wing things
And scaly wet fish things
And furry-skinned beast things."
And it was good.

So, that's what God did
with that nothing but nothing.
God turned it into something—
the biggest and best,
God made us a world, and put us right in it,
And then God was pleased
and decided to rest.
AND IT WAS VERY GOOD.

Based on Genesis 1:1-31.

Extending the story: Have the children choose a
favorite animal or plant to illustrate. Display the
pictures in the room to celebrate God's good
creation.

The Naming
by LeeDell Stickler

This story talks about how God directed Adam to name all the creatures. Talk about the children's names. Invite them to share their name. Point out that giving a name to a person or creature, gives it an identity. When it comes time to name the creatures, invite the children to supply the name. Read each description. Add more creatures if you have more time to fill.

Long ago when the world was brand new
God gave Adam a new job to do.
"Since none of my creatures is ever the same,
I think it is time that each had a name.
So, Adam invited the creatures to come.
Over mountains and deserts, they came, one by one.
Hopping and running and swimming they came.
And Adam gave each creature its very own name.

This creature has four legs and a long, bushy, striped tail. It's body is covered with thick fur. It looks like a bandit because it is always wearing a mask. I think I will call it _____. *(racoon)*

This creature has four legs and lives in family groups called prides. It has a long mane and a very loud roar. I think I will call it _____. *(lion)*

This creature has four legs and lives in the forests. It has thick fur and a long nose. It likes to eat honey and climb trees. I think I will call it _____. *(bear)*

This creature has no legs but can move very fast. It eats small animals. It makes a rattling sound to warn you to "beware." I think I will call it a_____. *(rattlesnake)*

This creature has only two legs. Its body is covered with bright feathers—red, blue, green, and yellow. This creature lives high in the trees of the tropical rain forest. I think I will call it a _____. *(parrot)*

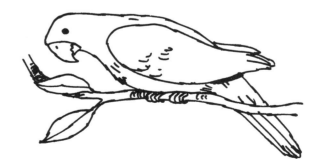

This creature has no legs at all and lives in the sea. It looks like a fish but it has lungs and breathes air. This creature is one of the largest creatures God created. I think I will call it a _____. *(whale)*

This creature has four legs and carries its house around on its back. It eats leaves and bugs. It moves very slowly. I think I will call it a _____. (turtle)

This creature has two very long legs. It is covered in bright pink feathers. It spends most of its time wading in water. I think I will call it a _____. (flamingo)

This creature has four legs and lives on the plains. It has a very long neck so that it can reach the topmost leaves of trees. This creature has brown spots on its body. I think I will call it a _____. (giraffe)

This creature has two legs and lives in caves and dark attics. It is covered with fur and flies. It makes a high pitched squeaking sound to locate objects. It drinks the nectar of some plants and eats primarily insects. This creature sleeps during the day and flies around at night. I think I will call it a _____. (bat)

This creature has eight legs and lives in the water. Its favorite home is in the ocean near a coral reef. This creature moves about by squirting jets of water. I think I will call it an _____. (octopus)

[Make up as many descriptions as you have the time and the children have the patience for.]

And so this is how each creature that is
Came by a name that is hers or is his.

Based on Genesis 2:18-20.

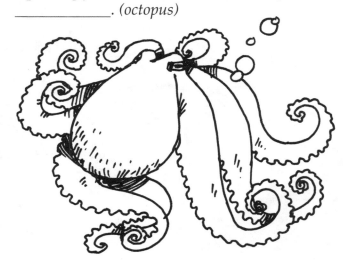

This creature has eight legs. It spins a web where it catches bugs for its dinner. I think I will call it a _____. (spider)

Extending the story: Have each child write his or her name on a piece of drawing paper. Encourage them to use large letters. Then let them decorate the letters.

Leaving the Garden
by LeeDell Stickler

Read the following story. When you get to the refrain, have the children pretend they are God talking to Adam and Eve. The children will stand do the following actions:

First line: *Point away from the body twice.*
Second line: *Shake finger.*
Third line: *Point away from the body twice.*
Fourth line: *Hands on hips, look annoyed.*
Fifth line: *Shake finger.*
Sixth line: *Extend arms away from body, palms up.*

Response:
Get out. Get out.
You didn't pay attention.
Get out. Get out.
I shouldn't have to mention,
That when I tell you what to do
There shouldn't be a question.

A long, long, long time ago when God created the world, God made a special garden. In this garden God placed the most wonderful plants and animals of every kind. It was in this garden that God placed the first man and the first woman. God called the man Adam. God called the first woman, Eve. God called the garden, Eden.

God said to Adam and Eve, "Take care of the plants and animals in my garden. You may eat from the fruit of all the trees in this garden except one. If you eat the fruit of the tree that grows in the center of the garden, you will die.

Response: (Whisper.)

Adam and Eve quickly agreed. After all, there were so many other things to eat that they could not even imagine eating from that special tree. And everything went well in the garden.

But one day Adam and Eve were walking through the garden. They passed through the center of the garden. There stood the special tree. It was so beautiful. The fruit looked so sweet and good. And they were both very hungry.

Response: (*Spoken in a normal voice.*)

Just then Eve heard a soft voice close to her ear. "Why don't you taste the fruit from the tree? It looks very good." Eve looked around and saw a snake wrapped around the tree branch. He smiled as only a snake could smile.

"It does look good. And I am sooooooo hungry," Eve agreed, "but God told us that if we ate from this tree we would die." The snake churckled. "What a silly thing to say! You will not die. This tree is very special. If you eat its fruit, you will become as wise as God. Don't you want to be as wise as God?"

Response: (*Spoken in a normal voice.*)

Eve thought for a moment. She wanted to do as God had told them. But she also wanted to be as wise as God. So, she picked a piece of fruit from the tree and took a big bite. Then she handed it to Adam, who also took a bite.

No sooner had they swallowed the bite of fruit than Eve and Adam knew they had done something terribly wrong.

"What will God say?" the two thought to themselves. They were soon to find out. God was angry. God was also very sad.

Response: (*Spoken slowly and sadly.*)

"I have created a special place for you to live. I have given you everything you could possibly want. And yet you have chosen to do the one th ing I told you not to do. For that reason, you cannot live in my special garden any longer. If you want to eat, you will have to grow your own food. You will have to farm. Life will be hard now. I gave you the freedom to choose, but you have chosen unwisely.

Extending the story: Bring in a variety of fruits and vegetables for the children to observe. Talk about how they grow and how they taste. Remind the children that God does provide for us.

Based on Genesis 2:4-3:24

Noah

The Story of Noah and the Ark
by LeeDell Stickler

Say: Since you were a small child, you have heard the story of Noah and the ark. This story tells us something very important about God. When all the storm was over and the earth was green and growing again, God made a promise to Noah and to all the people that were to come after him. And to this very day, God has kept that promise and will continue to keep that promise forever and ever and ever.

Teach the hand motions to the refrain:
1. Fingers together, touch right palm with left fingers. Reverse. Do this twice.
2. Hands above head, wiggled fingers as though rain falling as you lower hands.
3. Hands in fists. Arms bent at elbow held in front of the body. Make circles around one another.
4. Cross arms over chest. Extend arms out in front, palms up.

Refrain:
Drip, drop, pitter patter.
Raindrops fill the air.
Even though the thunder rolls,
God's love will still be there.

When God looked down upon the earth
And saw the evil there,
God thought the time had surely come
To start again down there.
God looked at all the people
Doing things that they should not
God looked for someone faithful
Some bright and shining spot.
It was then that God found Noah
A faithful man, and true,
Noah and his family lived
As God had told them to.

Refrain:

Noah, I'm not happy,
With things the way they are
I want to start all over,
So, you must build an ark.
Make it big and sturdy,
I'll tell you just what size,
For two of every creature,
Must be housed inside.
So Noah sawed and hammered
A boat of cypress wood.
He gathered all the animals in.
As God told him that he should.

Refrain:

There were elephants and ocelots,
Giraffes and kangaroos,
Lions, tigers, polar bears,
They came in two by two.
There were antelopes and cheetahs,
Ringed-tail cats and camels, too.
There were slinky snakes and turtles,
In Noah's floating zoo.
When two of every kind were there,
God closed them all in tight.
And soon the rain began to fall
For forty days and nights.

Refrain:

Splitter, slatter, dripety drop,
The rain fell on the boat.
Creak, crack, crickety, crunch.
The boat began to float.
The rain continued falling,
It covered up the land,
Soon there was nothing left to see,
But Noah's little band.
The ark rode on the water,
It floated to and fro,
It had no destination.
There was no place to go.

Refrain:

One day the rain did cease to fall,
The wind began to blow
The waters that had filled the earth,
Soon began to go.
The ark came to a resting place,
Atop of mountain high.
So through the open window,
Noah let a dove go fly.
"Fly around my little dove,
The sky is turning fair."
But soon the little dove returned
No place to land out there.

Refrain:

So Noah waited patiently,
Then sent the dove back out
What she brought back into the boat
Made Noah jump and shout.
She carried in her tiny beak,
A sign that there was spring,
The water-covered earth below,
Now had some growing things.
So Noah sent her out again
To look both east and west.
This time the dove did not return,
She'd found a place to nest.

Refrain:

Noah opened up the door,
The animals rushed outside,
What a sound these creatures made
Stompety, clompety, flutter, slide.
Then Noah built an altar,
Upon the muddy ground.
"We thank you God, most truly,
For keeping us safe and sound."
We thank you for giving us
A chance to start anew.
We'll try to live a better life
And do what we should do."

Refrain:

Then God spoke to Noah,
"Here's a promise to you from me.
I set my bow up in the clouds,
So you can clearly see.
I never will destroy the earth,
There'll always be a time,
Of planting and of harvesting,
On this world of mine.
My rainbow will remind you
Of the promise that we share,
That even though the thunder rolls,
My love will still be there."
Based on Genesis 6:9-9:17.

Abraham, Sarah, and their family

God Calls a People
by LeeDell Stickler

Teach the children the four line chant. At each point in the story, the children jump up from their chairs, quickly form a line, right hand on the left shoulder of the child in front of him or her and march around the room, repeating the verse. Select a new leader each time by having the child in front move to the back as quickly as possible. This might entail changing chairs. The children will listen for the key phrase—and they decided...

Refrain:
Wherever God may lead us,
Then that is where we'll go.
For we have put our trust in God,
God's always there, we know.

A long, long time ago, there was a man and his wife. Their names were Abraham and Sarah. One day God appeared to Abraham and said: "Abraham, I've got a plan. I want you and Sarah to pack up all your belongings and leave the land where you live right now. You are going to move to a land that I am going to show you. If you do this, then I will make from you and your children a great nation. Now, Abraham and Sarah didn't have any children just then. *But they decided...*
(Children march around the room.)

So, Abraham and Sarah packed up all their belongings and set off. First God led them here. Then God led them there. Life was not easy. And still Abraham and Sarah didn't know how they were going to be a great nation with just the two of them, a herd of sheep and goats, a few relatives and a bunch of servants. But they trusted God and *they decided...*
(Children march around the room.)

Finally God led Abraham and Sarah to Canaan. "This is the land that I promised you." God said. "You will have so many descendants that no one will be able to count them. They will be a many as the stars in the sky." Now Abraham was a very old man and so was Sarah. They were not sure just how God was going to do what God promised, but they knew that God was very powerful. *And they decided...*
(Children march around the room.)

So Abraham and Sarah settled into their new land. They had many, many sheep and goats. Their wealth was very great. But still they were only two—a few sheep and goats, and lots of nieces and nephews, but no children. Then one day, three visitors appeared at their tent. One of the visitors said, "This time next year, you and Sarah will have a son." Now Sarah, who had overheard the visitor began to laugh. For she was ninety years old. But the visitor said, "Remember, with God nothing is impossible." *And so they decided... (Children march around the room.)*

And what do you think happened? The very next year Abraham and Sarah had a son. They named him Isaac. And Abraham and Sarah did indeed become the beginning of a great nation—a nation of people who love God. And that nation is so large that they can scarcely be counted. And all this happened because *Abraham and Sarah decided... (Children march around the room.)*

Based on Genesis 12:1-9; 18:1-15; 21:1-8.

Twin Brothers

by LeeDell Stickler

To introduce the story, play a mirror game. Group the children in pairs, facing one another either sitting or standing. Select one child as A and one child as B. A will initiate a movement and let B try to imitate that movement exactly, as a mirror. Then swap and let B go first.

Say: Whenever we think of twins, we think of two people who are very much alike. But there are different kinds of twins. Some twins look exactly alike. Some twins look similar to one another. And some twins don't look alike at all. Today we will learn about two boys who, even though they were twins, were very different. Have the children continue to face each other. Between the verses of the poem, the children will do this:

Stomp right foot, stomp left foot
Pat right hand on right knee
Pat left hand on left knee
Clap hands together twice
Clap partners hands once.

Once there were twin brothers
As different as could be
And yet God had a plan for each
To be what each would be.
Stomp, stomp, pat, pat, clap, clap, clap

One brother truly liked to hunt
With an arrow and a bow.
He only liked to be outdoors
And go where he could go.
Stomp, stomp, pat, pat, clap, clap, clap

His hair was red and curly.
His skin was hairy too.
He was his father's favorite
Because of what he'd do.
Stomp, stomp, pat, pat, clap, clap, clap.

The second one did not go out.
He stayed around the tent.
He did not like to hunt wild game
He had a different bent.
Stomp, stomp, pat, pat, clap, clap, clap.

His hair was dark and straighter
Nothing like his brother
Because he liked to stay at home
He was loved best by his mother.
Stomp, stomp, pat, pat, clap, clap, clap.

Each brother had a gift
That he could call his own.
God had a plan for each of them
Whenever they were grown.
Stomp, stomp, pat, pat, clap, clap, clap.

Based on Genesis 25:19-26.
Read: Romans 12:6
(We have gifts that differ according to the grace given to us.)

The Blessing Thief

by LeeDell Stickler

Esau and Jacob may have been twins, but two different brothers there never have been. Esau was a hunter. (*Children stand up and imitate the strong man pose with arms bent and held in front.*) Jacob was a man of the tents who liked to cook. (*Children take both hands and pretend to stir a large stew and then taste it.*)

One day Jacob was cooking some bean soup when Esau came in from hunting. (*Children pretend to stir the stew and taste it.*) Esau was very hungry. (*Children rub stomachs.*)

"I'm starving. Give me some of that soup." (*Children extend right hand out palm up.*)

"Hmmm," thought Jacob. "I've got a plan." (*Children point index finger to right temple.*) "I'll give you what you want if you will give me your rights as the first born son." said Jacob. (*Children stroke chin shrewdly.*)

Even though the two boys were twins, Esau had been born first. He would be the one to inherit all of his father's property. Jacob didn't want to be left out.

"I am so hungry, what's a birthright if I die of starvation."(*Children scratch head as if Esau is thinking.*) "Done." said Esau, and Jacob handed his brother a bowl of soup. Esau did not know what he had done.

Many years later when he was very old and almost blind, Isaac, their father, called Esau over to him. (*Children make motioning signs with hands.*)

"Esau, before I die, I want to taste that stew you make. Then I will give you my final blessing." (*Children rub their stomachs.*)

So Esau hurried out to the fields to hunt for meat to make Isaac's favorite stew. (*Children march in place quickly.*)

"Jacob may have tricked me out of my birthright, but he will not trick me out of my father's blessing." (*Children shake index finger.*)

But Rebekah had been listening. (*Children put their right hand to ear.*) She had a plan. (*Children touch their index finger to temple.*)

"Jacob, I want you to have the blessing. I'll cook a stew. You give it to Isaac and pretend you are Esau. Then he will bless you instead."

"But father will know it isn't me. Esau is a hairy man. Father will know when he touches me." (*Children rub their arms as if feeling for hair.*)

So Rebekah dressed Jacob in goat skins. (*Children act as though they are putting on a coat.*) Jacob took the stew to his father. Isaac, thinking it was Esau, gave Jacob the final blessing. When Esau came home and discovered what had happened, he was very angry. (*Children make an angry face.*)

Jacob had to run away from home to keep Esau from hurting him. (*Children make running motions.*) Jacob was sad and he was afraid. (*Children cover face with hands.*)

But God said to him, "I love you and will be with you wherever you go." Jacob knew then that God had forgiven him even though he had cheated his brother.

Based on Genesis 25:27-34; 27:1-44

Jacob's Ladder
by LeeDell Stickler

Children will make climbing motions as though they are climbing the ladder between earth and sky.

When Jacob started on his journey
He felt so all alone.
He was going to a land
That was far away from home.

Refrain:
Climb, climb, climb the ladder.
(Make climbing motions as if climbing a ladder.)
Be brave and do not fear.
(Make muscle arms.)
Climb, climb, climb the ladder.
(Make climbing motions as if climbing a ladder.)
God is always near.
(Cross hands over chest.)

Soon the sun began to set.
Night clouds rolled and billowed.
Jacob lay down upon the ground
A stone served as his pillow.

Refrain:

Because the night was dark and cold
He pulled his mantle high
Jacob dreamed about a ladder
That went from earth to sky.

Up and down that golden path
That went from earth to heaven.
Angels came and angels went,
Four, five, six, and seven.

Refrain:

Then Jacob felt God's presence there
God spoke so loud and clear.
"I am with you always.
I am always near."

"The land on which you sleep is yours
And will forever be,
Your children will be many
From sea to sea to sea."

Refrain:

"Know that I am with you
No matter where you go.
I will bring you back here
That you'll surely know."

Then Jacob woke up from his sleep,
Amazement on his face.
He knew that he'd been sleeping in
The Lord's most holy place.

Refrain:

He built a special altar
And to God he made a vow
If God would love and keep him
He'd try much harder now.

Based on Genesis 28:10-22.

Joseph
by LeeDell Stickler

Have the children repeat each line after you, imitating the motions that you do.

Once a long time ago there lived a boy named Joseph. (*Thumbs hooked as if in suspenders.*)
Joseph had many brothers, all older than himself. (*Use hand to indicate height higher than self.*)
Except for Benjamin, who was younger. (*Use hand to indicate a smaller person.*)
But of all the sons, his father Jacob loved Joseph best of all. (*Lift chin; look haughty.*)
Jacob gave Joseph a marvelous coat. (*Turn around as if showing off special garment.*)
His brothers were very jealous. (*Put hands on hips; look annoyed.*)
But Joseph didn't care. (*Lift chin; look haughty.*)
One night Joseph had a dream. (*Put hands under chin as if asleep.*)
When he awoke he had to tell everyone about it. (*Jump up and down as if excited.*)
In my dream all of you bow down to me. (*Bow.*)
His brothers didn't like Joseph's dream. (*Hands on hips, look annoyed.*)
But Joseph didn't care. (*Lift chin; look haughty.*)
Another night Joseph had a dream. (*Put hands under chin as if asleep.*)
When he awoke he had to tell everyone about it. (*Jump up and down as if excited.*)
In my dream all of you bow down to me, even father and mother. (*Bow.*)
His brothers didn't like his dream. (*Hands on hips; look annoyed.*)
His father and mother didn't like his dream. (*Hands on hips; look annoyed.*)
But Joseph didn't care. (*Lift chin; look haughty.*)
Joseph's family had many sheep and goats. (*Pretend to pet a sheep.*)
Joseph's brothers watched them. (*Hand to forehead, look around.*)
One day Jacob sent Joseph out to check on his brothers. (*Point to the right.*)
They had been gone a long, long time. (*Count on fingers, one, two, three, four, five.*)
Jacob was worried about his sons. (*Wring hands.*)
So Joseph went. (*Walk; pretend to whistle.*)
His brothers saw him coming. (*Point to the left.*)
They were not happy. (*Hands on hips; look annoyed.*)
They decided to get rid of Joseph. (*Pretend to throw a large object.*)
When Joseph got near, they grabbed him. (*Act as though grabbing.*)
They took his coat. (*Pretend to remove coat.*)
They threw him into a dry well. (*Act as though throwing a large sack into the pit.*)
Then they sat down to eat their lunch. (*Dust hands off as if finished with a task.*)
Just then one brother saw a caravan of traders. (*Point off to the left.*)
"I've got an idea!" he said. (*Put finger to temple.*)
"We can get rid of Joseph and make some money, too." (*Act as though counting coins in palm of hand.*)
And so they sold Joseph to the traders. (*Wave goodbye to Joseph, blowing kisses.*)
They took his coat and dipped it in goat's blood. (*Act as though dipping coat.*)
They took it back to Jacob. (*Walk; whistling.*)
They told Jacob how a wild animal had killed his son. (*Pretend to cry.*)
Jacob was very sad. (*Pretend to cry even more, shoulders shaking.*)
Meanwhile, Joseph was on his way to Egypt. (*Walk; trudging.*)
He was sold as a slave to the captain of the guards. (*Act as though counting out money.*)
But God wasn't through with Joseph yet. (*Shake finger.*)

Based on Genesis 37.

Baby Moses
by LeeDell Stickler

Have the children use the hands motions for the verse.

Response:
Tiny basket on the river
(hands cupped together, rocking back and forth)
Baby Moses fast asleep
(hands together, tucked under side of face)
Sister Miriam in the rushes
(hands in front of face, fingers spread, peer through fingers)
A faithful watch she'll keep.
(Right and left hands to the side of the face, look to right and then to left)

Long, long ago in Bible times there lived a group of people. They were called Hebrews. They were God's chosen people. They came to live in the land of Egypt when a famine came to their land. They learned to be very happy there. And their number grew and grew and grew.

Soon, a new king came to the throne of Egypt. He was very cruel. He did not like the Hebrew people. In fact, the new king was afraid of them, because there were so many

of them. So he decided to make them work very, very hard.

"Perhaps if they had to work so hard, they would not have so many children," he thought to himself.

Response:

One day a baby boy was born into a Hebrew family. His mother and father were so happy. But they were worried. "The Pharaoh does not like us. The Pharaoh will not be pleased that we have a baby boy. We must hide the baby to keep him safe," said the baby's mother.

Soon the baby grew too big to hide. His laughter filled the house. So, the baby's mother made a basket out of grasses. She covered the outside of the basket with tar so that water could not get inside. She lined the inside of the basket with soft blankets. Then she tucked her baby inside and carried the basket to the river.

Response:

"Miriam," said the mother, "you must keep watch over your baby brother and keep him safe." So Miriam hid in the reeds on the bank of the river where she could see the basket."

Miriam had not been hiding very long when she heard voices. It was the pharaoh's daughter who had come to the river to take a bath. Miriam held her breath, hoping the princess would not see the little basket.

But as soon as the princess stepped into the water, she saw the basket. "Look, over there in the reeds," the princess pointed to where Miriam's brother was floating. "It looks like a basket. Bring it to me." One of the princess' maids waded into the water and got the basket.

Response:

The princess carefully opened the lid of the basket. "Oh," she exclaimed, when she saw what was inside. "What a beautiful baby! Some Hebrew mother has hidden her son here on the river to protect him from my father. I will take this baby and raise him as my very own son."

Just then Miriam had an idea. She jumped up from her hiding place and ran to the princess. "I could not help but hear what you said. You will need a nurse to care for your baby. I know just the person you need! Shall I get her for you?" The princess nodded. Miriam ran as fast as she could to her house.

Response:

"Mother, come quickly. The pharaoh's daughter has found our baby! I am to fetch a nurse for him." Miriam and her mother ran back to the river bank where the princess was holding the baby.

The princess held out the baby to his real mother. " Care for this baby and I will pay you," she said. "When he is older, you will bring him to the palace where he will live."

So the baby's mother took him home. There she loved him and cared for him with the princess' blessing. Then when he was old enough, she brought her son to the princess. The princess raised the baby as her very own son. The princess named him Moses, because it meant that he had been taken from the water.

Response:

Based on
  Exodus 1:8-2:8

Moses and the Burning Bush

by Raney Good

Have the children stand up and imitate the actions you do as you tell the story of Moses and the burning bush.

My name is Moses. I used to live in Egypt, but I made a big mistake and had to run away. Now I live in Midian. I work for Jethro, my father-in-law. I take care of his sheep. (*walk in place*)

Today, I took the sheep farther out into the wilderness, where the grass was better. As I was watching the sheep, I saw something unusual, high up on the hillside. (*hand above eyes, watch and point*)

There, on the side of the hill, a bush suddenly burst into flames. Now, grass fires are common in the wilderness. But as I looked closer (*peer with hand above eyes*), I saw that this was no ordinary fire. The bush was not being burned up. I thought to myself, "Maybe I should get a closer look." (*walk in place*)

So, I left my sheep in the valley and climbed up the hill. (*climbing motions*) As I got near the burning bush, a voice called out to me, "Moses, Moses! (*hand to ear*)

I stopped and looked around. (*look around*) But no one was there. Still, I answered, "Here I am!"

"Come no closer, Moses!" (*hand out in stopping motion*) the voice called out from within the bush. "Take off your sandals. You are standing on holy ground." I did as I was told. (*act out taking off shoes*)

The voice spoke again, "I am God. The God that your father and mother believe in. The God of your Hebrew family long ago— Abraham, Isaac, and Jacob."

Then I became afraid. I fell to my knees and hid my face. (*kneel down and hide face in arms*) God had never spoken to me before. I was afraid if I looked at God, something might happen to me.

Then God said, "I have heard my people in Egypt. They are crying to be free. (*hand to ear*) They need my help. I want you (*extend hand and point*) to go to Egypt and free my people. I want you (*extend hand and point*) to bring my people to a land that I have planned for them—a good land, a land where they will be happy."

"I cannot go back to Egypt," (*shaking head and crossing arms as a negative*) I thought to myself. But out loud I said, "I do not think I am right for this job. Surely someone else would be better."

But God said (*standing with hands on hips*), "Moses, you are the one I have chosen. I will show you what to do."

Based on Exodus 3:1-12.

Holy Moses Stomp
by Joyce Brown and Nancy Young

Make a copy of this reading for each child. Assign one group of children to be group 1 who will ask the question. Assign a second group of children to be group 2 who will be Moses responding.

Group 1: Baby Moses, where have you been?

Group 2: In a basket hiding from Pharaoh's men.

Group 1: Oh, yeah? *(Stomp, stomp)*

Group 2: Oh yeah! *(Stomp, stomp)*

Group 1: Grown-up Moses, what is that sound?

Group 2: The crackle of flames on holy ground.

Group 1: Oh, yeah?
(Stomp, stomp)

Group 2: Oh yeah!
(Stomp, stomp)

Group 1: Stubborn Moses, what did God ask?

Group 2: For me to do an impossible task.

Group 1: Oh, yeah?
(Stomp, stomp)

Group 2: Oh yeah!
(Stomp, stomp)

Group 1: Leader Moses, what did you do?

Group 2: God parted the sea; I led them through.

Group 1: Oh, yeah?
(Stomp, stomp)

Group 2: Oh yeah!
(Stomp, stomp)

Group 1: Brother Moses, what do you see?

Group 2: My sister dancing because we're free.

Group 1: Oh, yeah?
(Stomp, stomp)

Group 2: Oh yeah!
(Stomp, stomp)

Group 1: Troubled Moses, what's all the fuss?

Group 2: My people are acting ridiculous.

Group 1: Oh, yeah?
(Stomp, stomp)

Group 2: Oh yeah!
(Stomp, stomp)

Group 1: Holy Moses, what have you got?

Group 2: Some rules from God that help a lot.

Group 1: Oh, yeah?
(Stomp, stomp)

Group 2: Oh yeah!
(Stomp, stomp)

Group 1: Holy Moses, what do you know?

Group 2: Following God is the way to go!

Group 1: Oh, yeah?
(Stomp, stomp)

Group 2: Oh yeah!
(Stomp, stomp)

Based on Exodus.

Let My People Go
by Myrtle Felkner

Have the children "sing" the response. If you do not know the tune, simply say the phrase.

Leader: Moses and Aaron went to Pharaoh and asked that the Israelites be permitted to leave Egypt to worship God. But Pharaoh responded by making the work of the slaves even harder than before. Finally God told Moses, "Now you shall see what I will do to Pharaoh" (Exodus 6:1). And as the Lord commanded, Moses and Aaron struck the waters of the Nile and all the waters of Egypt turned to blood (7:20).

(*Children sing or sign*)
"Let my people go!"

Leader: But Pharaoh would not let the people go. According to the Lord's command "frogs came up and covered the land of Egypt." (8:6)

(*Children sing or sign*)
"Let my people go!"

Leader: But Pharaoh would not let the people go. "Aaron . . . struck the dust of the earth, and . . . all the dust of the earth turned into gnats throughout the whole land of Egypt." (8:17)

(*Children sing or sign*)
"Let my people go!"

Leader: "Great swarms of flies came . . . in all of Egypt the land was ruined because of the flies." (8:24)

(*Children sing or sign*)
"Let my people go!"

Leader: "All of the livestock of the Egyptians died." (9:6)

(*Children sing or sign*)
"Let my people go!"

Leader: "So they took soot from the kiln . . .

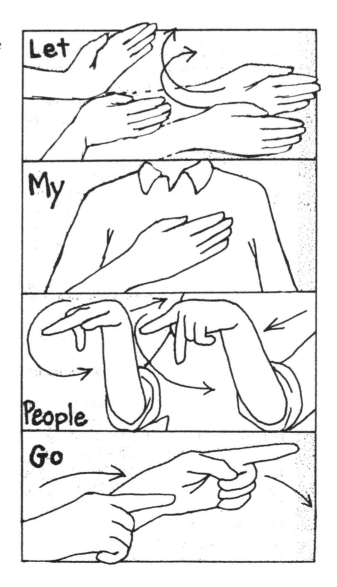

and Moses threw it in the air, and it caused festering boils on humans and animals." (9:10)

(*Children sing or sign*)
"Let my people go!"

Leader: "And the Lord rained hail on the land of Egypt; . . . hail with fire flashing continually in the midst of it." (9:23-24)

(*Children sing or sign*)
"Let my people go!"

Leader: "Locusts came upon all the land of Egypt, . . . They covered the surface of the whole land." (10:14-15)

(*Children sing or sign*)
"Let my people go!"

Leader: So Moses stretched out his hand toward heaven, and there was dense darkness in all the land of Egypt for three days." (10:22)

(*Children sing or sign*)
"Let my people go!"

Leader: "At midnight the Lord struck down all the firstborn in the land of Egypt." (12:29)

(*Children sing or sign*)
"Let my people go!"

Then at last Pharaoh said, "Take your flocks and your herds . . . and be gone!" (12:32) That very day the Lord brought the Israelites out of the land of Egypt.

Based on Exodus 4:20—5:9, 22-23; 6:1; 7:14—12:32; 12:41

In the Wilderness
by Raney Good

Have the children do the actions after each group of sentences.

Free at last! Free at last!
God's people were free at last!
(*Shake hands overhead in praise.*)

Now God was leading the Hebrew people
into the desert on their
way to the Promised Land.
(*Walk with hand to forehead.*)

They traveled a long, long time.
(*Walk slower, more tired.*)

And they became thirsty, oh so thirsty!
(*Stop and put hands to throat.*)

But there was no water to be found.
(*Put hand above eyes, looking around.*)

"Moses this is all your fault. Do something!"
(*Put hand on hip and shake a finger.*)

Moses did not know what to do.
(*Shrug shoulders.*)

So, Moses turned to God for help.
(*Hold arms up.*)

And God told Moses just what to do.
(*Cup hand to ear.*)

"Moses take your staff and strike that rock!"
(*Pretend staff hits rock.*)

Water squirted! Water gushed!
Water, water, everywhere!
(*Make fountain motions with hands.*)

There was water for everyone to drink! (*Cup
hands and act like drinking.*)

And the people went on their way, looking
for the Promised Land.
(*Walk with hand to forehead.*)

They traveled a long, long time.
(*Walk slower, more tired.*)

Soon they became hungry, oh so hungry!
(*Stop and put hands to stomach.*)

But there was no food to be found.
(*Put hand above eyes, looking around..*)

And the people were very unhappy.
(*Make sad faces.*)

"We're hungry, Moses, and it's all your fault.
Do something! they shouted.
(*Put hand on hip, shaking finger.*)

Moses knew just what to do.
(*Hold up arms in prayer.*)

God would provide whatever they needed.
(*Look around.*)

That night some quail landed nearby.
(*Make flapping motions with hands and arms.*)

They were tired and slow.
They made a great supper.
(*Rub stomach, nod head.*)

The next morning God again provided food.
(*Make a surprised face.*)

There was something like
bread all over the ground.
(*Point all around.*)

And God said, "Take only
what you need for each day.
(*Pick up bread from ground.*)

And a little extra for your day of rest."
(*Pick up bread from ground.*)

Wherever the Hebrew people went,
God took care of them.
(*Hold arms up.*)

Based on Exodus 15:22-17:7.

The Ten Commandments
by LeeDell Stickler

Photocopy this reading. Assign a child to each Reader part. The Narrator will read the biblical text and the child will read a paraphrase.

Narrator: I am the Lord your God, who brought you out of the land of Egypt, out of the house of slavery, you shall have no other gods before me.

Reader 1: I will worship only God.

Narrator: You shall not make for yourself an idol. You shall not bow down to them or worship them.

Reader 2: I will worship only God.

Narrator: You shall not make wrongful use of the name of the Lord your God.

Reader 3: I will use God's name in a respectful way.

Narrator: Remember the Sabbath day and keep it holy.

Reader 4: I will set aside one day to rest and to remember all that God has done.

Narrator: Honor your father and mother.

Reader 5: I will show respect for my parents.

Narrator: You shall not murder.

Reader 6: I will not intentionally kill anyone.

Narrator: You shall not commit adultery.

Reader 7: When I get married, I will be faithful to my wife or husband.

Narrator: You shall not steal.

Reader 8: I will not take things that do not belong to me.

Narrator: You shall not bear false witness against your neighbor.

Reader 9: I will say only truthful things about other people.

Narrator: You shall not covet your neighbor's house; you shall not covet your neighbor's wife; or anything that belongs to your neighbor.

Reader 10: I will not want to have what my neighbor has.

Based on Exodus 20:1-17.

Building a House for God

(A Reading Play)
by Myrtle Felkner

Setting: in front of an Israelite family tent, camped near Mt. Sinai

Characters:
an Elder of the tribe
several boys and girls
Bezalel
Oholiab

Elder: Our tent of worship is almost completed! We have a fantastic tabernacle here in the desert. Bezalel*, and Oholiah*, you have done great work.

Bezalel: Of course God gave us the skills we needed. When God told Moses to put me in charge of the workmen, I knew why God had blessed me with building and artistic skills.

Elder: Yes, God certainly had a plan.

Oholiab: Everyone whose spirit was joyful brought materials to use in the sanctuary. It's not hard to build when you have such enthusiastic people!

Elder: Even some of these children brought gifts.

First child: I had an onyx* that lady in Egypt gave me when we left. I was glad to give it! Moses said Oholiab would use it in the tabernacle.

Second child: And I had a wooden box made from acacia*. Moses said we would need a lot of acacia wood I the tabernacle, so I gave it right away.

Third child: My mother has been busy for weeks. She and the other women sing all day as they weave the big tent of goats' hair to cover the tabernacle.

Fourth child: Bezalel, how did you know how to make the tabernacle? Did Moses figure it all out?

Bezalel: Oh, no! When Moses was on Mt. Sinai, God told him exactly how to make the tabernacle, down to the last little bit of embroidery. At first I wondered how we would ever get all that done!

Elder: I wondered where we were going to find gold and silver and fine twisted linen and red dye. We had been gone from Egypt almost a year.

First child: I know, I know! We carried it out of Egypt. That's why God caused the Egyptians to give us their jewelry and other fine stuff as we left.

Oholiab (*chuckling*)**:** Then a funny problem came up. After we got started, the people still came every morning with more gold and more silver and more acacia wood. We had too much! We had to ask Moses to tell the people not to bring any more offerings.

Second child: I guess it's like the manna, the water, and the quails. God makes sure that we have what we need.

Elder: Now we have a beautiful tent of worship that we can carry with us when we move to the Promised Land of our ancestors. God will go before us if we trust God and are obedient!

*Bezalel (BEZ-uh-el) onyx (ON-iks)
 Oholiab (oh-HOH-lee-ab)
 acacia (uh-KAY-shuh)

Based on Exodus 35:4—36:7

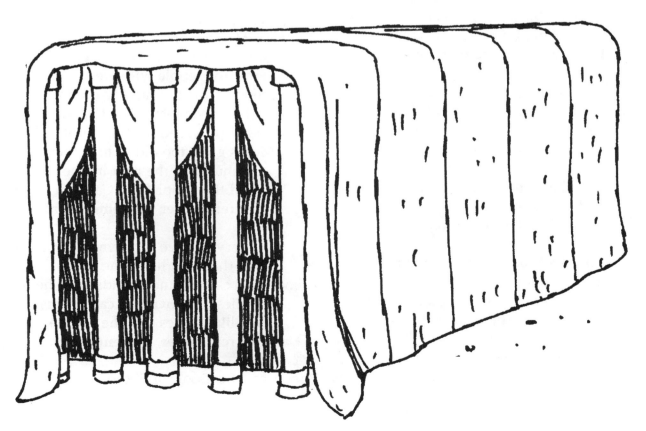

The Story of Moses
by LeeDell Stickler

Prepare phrase cards for the children. Choose as many phrase cards as you have children. These are possible phrase cards:
Baby Moses/in a basket/With the princess/in the palace/Called by God/Free my people/the mighty pharaoh/Led his people/'cross the sea/God provided/too old to lead them/next in line/into Canaan.
When the children hear their phrase, they stand up until the poem comes to the phrase, We remember, we remember. Then everyone sits down and starts again.

Moses' mother placed her baby
In a basket in the river.
Pharaoh's daughter found the basket
Took the baby for her own.
Baby Moses in a basket,
With the princess.
We remember, we remember.

Moses grew up in the palace,
Raised as Pharaoh's daughter's son.
Moses made a big mistake
Had to run away one day.
Baby Moses in a basket,
With the princess in the palace,
Had to run away one day.
We remember, we remember.

God called Moses back to Egypt,
"Free my people who are slaves."
Moses stood before the pharaoh,
With his brother Aaron, too.
Baby Moses in a basket,
With the princess in the palace,
Had to run away one day.
Called by God back into Egypt,
"Free my people who are slaves."

Stood before the mighty pharaoh.
We remember, we remember.

Moses led the Hebrew people
Out of Egypt, 'cross the sea.
God provided for the people,
Meat and bread and water, too.
Baby Moses in a basket,
With the princess in the palace
Had to run away one day.
Called by God back into Egypt.
"Free my people who are slaves."
Stood before the mighty pharaoh.
Led his people 'cross the sea.
God provided for the people.
We remember, we remember.

Moses grew too old to lead them,
Joshua was the next in line.
Joshua led the Hebrew people
To the land that God had planned.
Baby Moses in a basket,
With the princess in the palace,
Had to run away one day.
Called by God back into Egypt.
"Free my people who are slaves."
Stood before the mighty pharaoh.
Led his people 'cross the sea.
God provided for the people.
Moses grew too old to lead them.
Joshua was the next in line.
Led the people into Canaan.
We remember, we remember.

Every day we can remember
All that God has done for us.
Food and clothes and friends and shelter,
Families that love and care for us.
Just like Moses and the people,
We remember, we remember.

Based on the Book of Exodus

The Falling Walls
by LeeDell Stickler

Create cue cards on index cards or posterboard. Put one of these words or phrases on each card: Hebrew people, city of Jericho, Joshua, priests.

Say: I'm going to let you help me tell a story. Each of you will have a part. When I hold up the card that has that part on it, you will do a certain action.

Hebrew people: *stand up and march in place*
City of Jericho: *link arms and form a wall*
Joshua: *stand tall and straight and salute*
Priests: *fists to mouth, make a trumpet sound*

For forty years the HEBREW PEOPLE had wandered in the wilderness. Moses had grown very old. JOSHUA was now the leader. God decided that the time was right to enter the promised land. At the entry to the Promised Land there stood a great city—the CITY OF JERICHO. It was a large city with great high walls all around it to protect it. If the HEBREW PEOPLE were to enter the Promised Land, they had to capture the CITY OF JERICHO.

"Hmmmm," JOSHUA thought to himself. "The CITY OF JERICHO is surrounded by a great wall. It is too high to climb. It is too strong to knock down. The gates are tightly closed. It is impossible to capture this city."

But God said to JOSHUA, "I've got a plan. But you must follow it exactly as I tell you, even if it may seem strange to you. First you will march around the CITY OF JERICHO one time, with all the soldiers. The HEBREW PEOPLE should not make a single sound. Do this every day for six days. On the seventh day, you will march around the CITY OF JERICHO seven times. As you march, the PRIESTS will blow their horns. At a special signal, the PRIESTS will make one long, loud blast on the horns. At that time I want all the HEBREW PEOPLE to shout as loud as they can. The walls of the CITY OF JERICHO will fall down.

So, JOSHUA told the HEBREW PEOPLE what God had told him to do. "We must do just as God said."

The HEBREW PEOPLE marched quietly around the city. (Have the children get up and march around the circle.) The people from inside the CITY OF JERICHO looked out at the silent army. "What was going on?" they wondered. Five more days the HEBREW people marched silently around the CITY OF JERICHO and returned to their camp. *(March the children around the room five more times.)*

Everyone was beginning to wonder what was going to happen. On the seventh day, the HEBREW PEOPLE marched around the CITY OF JERICHO one time, two times, three times, four times, five times, six times, seven times, just as JOSHUA had told them. The PRIESTS blew the horns as they marched. Then after the seventh time around the PRIESTS blew one loud long blast on the hornes. JOSHUA gave the signal. The HEBREW PEOPLE shouted. *(Have the children shout.)*

What a loud noise there was. Then, everyone watched as the walls of the CITY OF JERICHO began to crack and crumble and rumble and roar. Just as God had promised, the walls of the CITY OF JERICHO fell down flat. *(Have the children fall down to the ground.)*

Based on Joshua 6.

David and Solomon

David and Goliath
by LeeDell Stickler

Read the following story with the children. By the time you reach the end of the story, the children will be repeating the highlighted sentence with you.

Long ago in a land far away there lived a boy named David. David had eight brothers. Each of his brothers was older, and bigger, and stronger than David. Whenever there was important work to be done, David's brothers always did it.

"You are too young," said one. "You are too small," said another. "You are not nearly strong enough," said a third. But David knew that what they were really saying was "You are not very important."

David knew better. "I may be little, but with God's help I can do important things."

While David's brothers were off doing other jobs, David cared for his family's sheep. David thought this was a very important job. He helped the sheep find green grass and fresh cool water. He kept the sheep from wandering off into dangerous paths. With his trusty sling, he protected his flock from lions and wolves and bears. At the end of the day when David brought the sheep together into the sheep fold, he would say to God. "Thank you God for helping me be a good shepherd."

And David said to himself, "I may be little, but with God's help I can do important things."

One day his father called him in from the field. "David, I have a job for you to do. Your brothers are soldiers in King Saul's army. I have not heard from them in a long time. Take some food to them. Bring back news of how they are," said his father.

David felt very important. The journey was long and dangerous and so David asked God to help him travel safely.

And when he set off, David said to himself, "I may be little, but with God's help I can do important things."

David came to where the two armies were lined up against one another. King Saul's army was in the valley. The Philistine army was on the hillside. Both sides were ready for battle. David hurriedly found his brothers.

Just then a soldier stepped from the ranks

of the other army. He was huge—bigger than any man David had ever seen. The soldier held his sword high in the air. "My name is Goliath! Why should armies fight this battle? Choose a man from your side. Let him come down to fight me. Whoever wins, wins the war." No one came forward. Everyone was frightened of Goliath.

"Who is this man that frightens the army of God?" asked David. "Why doesn't someone go forward and fight him?

"If you are so brave, then why don't you do it?" his brothers teased him.

"All right, I will. I'm not afraid. **I may be little, but with God's help I can do important things."** said David.

David's brothers brought him to King Saul. They told the king what David had said. King Saul shook his head. "You cannot fight this soldier. You are too young. You are too little. You are too weak," said the king.

But David said, "I am stronger than I look. Since I was a young boy, I have cared for my father's sheep. With my sling, I have killed a lion and a bear who attacked my sheep. God who saved me from the lion and the bear will save me from Goliath."

King Saul gave David his helmet, his armor, and his sword. But they were so heavy that David could hardly walk. "I will fight this man with just my sling and five smooth stones." said David.

So, David went out to meet Goliath. A gasp of surprise came from both armies. Who was this young boy? How could he be the one to fight Goliath?

When Goliath saw David coming, he began to laugh. He laughed and laughed and laughed. "You are too young. You are too little. You are too weak. I will make bird food of you!" Goliath shouted at the boy.

"I may be young. I may be little. I may be weak. But with God's help I can do important things." David thought to himself.

But out loud he said, "You may have a sword and a shield, but I stand here in the name of God."

David prayed to God that he would be brave. He reached into his bag and pulled out a smooth stone. David placed the stone in the pocket of his sling. He swung the sling over his head, around and around and around. Then, he let it go. The stone flew through the air and struck Goliath on the forehead. Goliath fell to the ground.

Everyone was surprised, but not David. **"I may be young. I may be little. I may be weak. But with God's help I can do important things."**

Based on 1 Samuel 17:12-54.

Extend the story: Let your children act out the story of David and Goliath.

David and Jonathan

(A Play)

by Linda Whited

Narrator: After David came to live in his court, Saul let David lead part of his army. David was a good leader. At first Saul was happy. But then people started calling David a hero and paying more attention to him than to King Saul. King Saul was jealous. He made plans to get rid of David.

Jonathan: David, you are my very best friend. We are like brothers. I wish my father liked you.

David: I don't mean to make King Saul mad. I'm just doing what God wants me to do.

Narrator: But King Saul kept hearing good things about David, and King Saul got angrier and angrier. "I am going to get rid of that David," he said. "Maybe then people will pay more attention to me!"

Jonathan: David, David! I overheard my father. He's planning to hurt you. I've come to warn you.

David: What should I do?

Jonathan: Be on guard tomorrow morning. Stay in a secret place and hide. I will talk to my father. Maybe I can change his mind.

Narrator: The next day Jonathan talked to his father. He explained that David had done nothing wrong. King Saul promised that he would not hurt David.

Jonathan: David, my father has said that he will not hurt you.

David: Thank you, Jonathan. Thank you for being my friend and standing up for me.

Narrator: But King Saul soon forgot his promise. David had to run away from Saul.

David: Jonathan, what have I done to make King Saul so angry? Why is he trying to kill me?

Jonathan: Surely you are wrong, David. My father promised not to hurt you. But I will find out. Hide in the field. I will come with a message. No matter what happens, though, please remain a faithful friend to me and my family forever.

David: I promise! I will always love you and care for your family.

Narrator: Jonathan found out that David was right. King Saul did want to kill David. So the next day he went to the field to warn his friend. They both cried and hugged one another.

Jonathan: Go in peace, David. May the Lord be with us and with our descendants forever!

Based on 1 Samuel 18:1-16; 19:1-7; 20:1-42.

David the King

(A Reading Play)
by Linda Whited

Narrator: Saul was king as long as he lived. But Saul was unfaithful to God, and God began to make plans for choosing a new king to follow Saul. God sent Samuel to Bethlehem to choose one of Jesse's sons to become king.

Samuel: I come in peace. I am here to make a sacrifice. You may join me if you wish. Invite Jesse and his family to come.

Narrator: Samuel prepared for the sacrifice as everyone gathered. When the time came, Samuel spoke to Jesse.

Samuel: Jesse, God has chosen the next king from among your sons. Bring your sons to me. God will tell me which one has been chosen.

Narrator: Each of Jesse's sons passed before Samuel; but each time God said, "No, this is not the one."

Samuel (aside to himself): I was sure that Eliab was the Lord's anointed one. But God said, "No."

Samuel: Jesse, none of these is the one the Lord has chosen. Do you have another son who is not here?

Jesse: Yes, but he is the youngest one, the smallest one, only a child. Surely he is not the one the Lord will choose. He is not here because he is taking care of the sheep.

Samuel: God has said, "Do not judge by how he looks or how tall he is." It's clear. God does not judge by outward appearance. God looks on the heart. Send for your son David. We will not begin the feast until he comes.

Narrator: So David was brought quickly from the fields and taken to Samuel.

Samuel: There is no question. This son is the next king, for God has said, "Rise and anoint him; for this is the one."

Narrator: So Samuel took the horn of oil and anointed David in the presence of his father and his brothers. The spirit of the Lord came upon David and stayed with him for the rest of his life.

Based on 1 Samuel 16:1-13.

King Solomon's Temple

(A Reading and Action Play)
by Linda Whited

Have the children perform the actions as you tell the story.

"**S**oon you will be king," David said to his son Solomon. (*Form a crown on head with hands.*)

"You must be strong." (*Flex arm muscles.*)

"You must have courage." (*Flex arm muscles.*)

"And most of all, you must obey God." (*Put palms together on chest and bow head.*)

Narrator: And when God asked King Solomon what gift he would want, Solomon asked for wisdom, and an understanding mind, to rule the people wisely. God was pleased and gave Solomon more wisdom than any king had ever had before.

King Solomon said, "I will build a house for God. I will build the Temple my father dreamed of." (*Form a roof with both arms.*)

It will be a place where people can worship. (*Put palms together on chest and bow head.*)

Narrator: King Solomon asked King Hiram of Tyre to provide cedars of Lebanon. Only the best lumber was good enough for the house of the Lord. King Hiram supplied King Solomon's every need.

Finally the temple was ready. (*Spread out arms and smile.*)

Narrator: The Temple was magnificent. It was made of stone and lined with cedar. (*Smell the cedar.*) The inner portion of the building was inlaid with gold. Great bronze columns stood at the front. There were carvings of palm trees, olive trees, and opened flowers. A special place was prepared for the ark of the covenant.

The people gathered to worship God. (*Put palms together on chest and bow head.*)

They lifted the ark of the covenant and carried it into the Temple. (*Grip hands above right shoulder as if holding a pole on the ark.*)

Then Solomon made an offering to God and blessed the people of Israel. (*Put palms together on chest and bow head.*)

Narrator: And so the promise God made to David was fulfilled. David's son Solomon built a house for the Lord, the God of Israel.

Based on 1 Kings 2:1-4, 3:1-14; 5:1-12; 8:1-15.

© 1995 Cokesbury.

Kings and Prophets

The Story of Nehemiah
by LeeDell Stickler

This story is told in a similar fashion to the old nursery rhyme "The House that Jack Built." It is a cumulative action story. You will need six groups of children. (*One child can be a group.*)

1. **The wall:** *Stand with arms outstretched.*
2. **The stones:** *Arms forming a circle in front.*
3. **The people:** *Hands on the hips.*
4. **Enemies:** *Hold up fists as though ready to fight.*
5. **Guards:** *Hold one arm as if holding a shield, the other as if holding up a sword.*
6. **The community:** *Stand up arms outstretched, turn around.*

Assign each child to a group. Children will listen for the phrase that indicates what they are. When the story comes to their part, the children in that group stand up, do the action, and then immediately sit down. The faster you say the story, the more fun it will be. Do the story several times.

This is the wall that Nehemiah built.
(*Children who are the wall stand up.*)

These are the stones that made up the wall that Nehemiah built.
(*Stones and wall stand up.*)
These are the people who placed the stones in the wall that Nehemiah built.
(*People, stones, and wall stand up.*)
These are the enemies who bothered the people who placed the stones in the walls that Nehemiah built.
(*Enemies, people, stones, and wall stand up.*)

These are the guards who watched for the enemies who bothered the people who placed the stones in the wall that Nehemiah built.
(*Guards, enemies, people, stones, and wall stand up.*)

This is the community that grew from the guards who watched for the enemies who bothered the people who placed the stones in the wall that Nehemiah built.
(*All groups stand.*)

Based on Nehemiah 2:4-6, 11-18; 12:27-43.

Nehemiah
(An Echo Story)
by Mary Jane Pierce-Norton

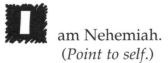 am Nehemiah.
(*Point to self.*)

One day I heard that the walls of Jerusalem
were all torn down.
(*Cup hand to ear.*)

This made me sad.
(*Rub eyes.*)

I prayed to God.
(*Clasp hands together.*)

"Dear God, I want to go to Jerusalem and
help rebuild the walls.
(*Pretend to stack blocks and to hammer.*)

Please be with me. Amen."
(*Clasp hands together.*)

Then I went to the emperor to ask for permission to go to Jerusalem.
(*Walk in place.*)

The emperor listened to me. He gave me
what I needed for the trip.
(*Stretch out hands in front
as if to be giving something away.*)

I went to Jerusalem.
(*Walk in place.*)

I inspected the walls of the city.
(*Walk in place and look
to the left and to the right.*)

Then I called the people together.
(*Motion toward self.*)

"Together we can rebuild the walls," I said.
(*Reach down to the ground, then
reach above your head.*)

So we all worked to rebuild the walls of
Jerusalem.
(*Use hands to show stacking bricks for the walls.*)

When we finished the walls, we were glad.
We celebrated!
(*Point to face and smile.*)

We thanked God for helping us.
(*Clasp hands in prayer.*)

Based on Nehemiah 1:1—2:20; 6:15-16.

Huldah Spoke God's Word

(A Play)

by Myrtle Felkner

Cast of Characters:
Shaphan: *Secretary to the king*
King Josiah
Huldah: *Prophetess*
Hilkiah: *Priest*

Scene 1: In the palace

Shaphan: King Josiah, everything has been done as you said. Hilkiah, the high priest, has turned over the money to the workers to repair the temple. But there is one disturbing thing.

Josiah: What is that?

Shaphan: Hilkiah has found a book of the law hidden in the house of the Lord. Here it is.

Josiah: Wonderful! Read it! Read it! We will see what the Lord has said to our ancestors.

(*Some time later*)

Josiah: How great is our sin! My grandfather and my father have sinned against the Lord God, and they have led all of Judah to sin against the Lord. Shaphan, send for Hilkiah and for my servants! You must all go to ask the Lord what these words mean. God is very angry with us!

Scene 2: At Huldah's home

Huldah: You have come to seek a word from God?

Hilkiah: While repairing the Temple, the workmen found this lost book.

Shaphan: I have read it to the king. He is weeping and tearing his clothing in grief that our people have sinned and turned from God. What is to be done?

Hilkiah: The words of the Law in this book are severe. Can it be that God will cause Judah to fall? King Josiah wishes to make amends before God for the wickedness of his ancestors.

Huldah: Tell the king that this is the word from God—the sins of Judah have been very bad. God will indeed punish the nation, just as this lost book says. Judah has not kept the covenant made with God.

Hilkiah: Shaphan, write this down to tell the king.

Huldah: Tell the king this also. God has heard his prayers and seen his grief because of this sin. God has seen how the king humbled himself and repented of the actions of his ancestors. Josiah will not see the disaster that will come to Judah. God will allow him to die in peace before that time comes.

Scene 3: At the palace

Josiah: We will make amends as far as possible. Gather all the people before me to hear the words of the Law. We will strike down the altars to false gods. We will turn our hearts to the true God!

Based on 2 Kings 22:1—23:27.

Jonah, Esther, Daniel, Ruth

Jonah and the Big Fish
by LeeDell Stickler

Read the following story. Emphasize the poem response after each narrative section. By the end of the story, the children will be saying it with you. Involve the children by pausing before you read the last word and let the children supply it.

Once a long time ago, there lived a man named Jonah. Jonah was a good man. Jonah obeyed all the laws. Jonah tried do everything that God wanted him to do.

And Jonah said:
I want to always do what's right
I want to be faithful and true.
I try to live as God would want
And do what God wants me to.

One day God spoke to Jonah. "Jonah, I want you to go to the grand city of Nineveh. Tell the people there how wicked they are. I want them to change their wicked ways or they will be very sorry."

And Jonah said:
I always want to do what's right
I want to be faithful and true.
I try to live as God would want
But this I will not do.

Jonah did not like the people of Nineveh. They were his enemies. Jonah didn't care what God did to the people who lived there. So, instead of going to Nineveh, Jonah bought a ticket for a ship that was going in the opposite direction.

And Jonah said:
I always want to do what's right.
I want to be faithful and true.
But now I'm going to run away,
That's just what I will do.

So, Jonah got onto the ship. He went below and promptly fell asleep. While Jonah was sound asleep, the boat set sail. As it sailed, a great storm came up. The wind blew. The lightning flashed. The waves crashed against the ship. Everyone feared the boat would sink.

The captain woke Jonah up. "How can you sleep in such a storm? Pray to your God that we might not all be killed."

And Jonah said:
I always want to do what's right.
I want to be faithful and true.
But when I ran away from God,
I brought this trouble for you.

So, Jonah told the sailors, "Throw me into the sea and the storm will come to an end." The sailors did not want Jonah to drown. So, instead, they rowed with all their might. But the storm just got worse and worse.

Again Jonah said:
I always want to do what's right.
I want to be faithful and true.
Throw me into the deep dark sea
That's just what you must do.

Finally, the sailors picked Jonah up and threw him over the side. As soon as Jonah hit the water, the storm stopped. Jonah would have drwned. But God sent from the deep dark depths of the ocean a big fish. The fish opened its mouth and swallowed Jonah whole.

And Jonah said:
I always want to do what's right.
I want to be faithful and true.
Now here I am in the belly of a fish,
Feeling sad and blue.

For three days Jonah sat there in the belly of that fish. For three days Jonah thought about what he had done. For three days Jonah prayed to God.

And Jonah said:
I always want to do what's right.
I want to be faithful and true.
Whatever job you have for me,
Then that is what I'll do.

The fish came to the surface of the water and spit Jonah onto the dry land. Again God spoke to Jonah, "Jonah, I want you to go to the grand city of Nineveh. Tell the people there how wicked they are. I want them to change their ways or they will be very sorry."

And do you know what Jonah did? He went. And do you know what the people of Nineveh did? They changed their ways.

Based on Jonah 1-3.

Daniel and the Lions
by Alice Ann Glenn

Let the children create lion puppets (*See example.*) from lunch-sized paper bags. Let them participate as the lions from the story.

Say: I am going to tell the story, but I need your help. Every time you hear the word FAITHFUL, I want to hear the lions roar. Let me hear you roar. (*Let the children roar.*) **You don't sound hungry enough. Let me hear you roar again.**

Once, a long, long time ago, in a land very far away, there was a king named Darius. This king had many court officials who helped him to run the country. One of these court officials was a man named Daniel. Unlike the other court officials, Daniel was an honest man and a hard worker. He was **faithful** to God.

Because Daniel was such a hard worker, the king made Daniel head of all the other court officials. This did not make these officials very happy. In fact, they were very jealous. They began to look for a way to make Daniel look bad in the eyes of the king. But as hard as they tried, they could find nothing wrong with Daniel. Daniel was kind and good and honest. Daniel was **faithful** to his God.

Then, one day, one of the court officials had an idea. "If we are going to get Daniel in trouble, it will have to do with his faith in his God. I have seen him go up to his room three times a day to pray to God. Suppose we have the king make a law that says it is illegal to pray to anyone but the king. Daniel will

never follow such a law. He is very **faithful** to his God."

The court officials went to the king. "O King Darius, may you live forever. We have decided that you should make a special law. No one is to pray to anyone except the king for the next thirty days. Anyone who breaks the law will be thrown into a den of hungry lions. And this law will be one that even the king cannot break."

"Done!" said the king and he signed the law into being. The court officials smiled little secret smiles. Now they wondered just what **faithful** Daniel would do.

Daniel knew about the new law. But Daniel was **faithful** to God. And God's law said that

Daniel was to pray to God three times a day and to pay to no one else. Daniel certainly didn't want to disobey the king's law, but he also didn't want to disobey God's law either. So just as he had always done, three times a day, **faithful** Daniel went to his room to pray. This pleased the court officials. Because now, they knew, that they could get Daniel into trouble.

When the officials told the king what Daniel was doing, the king was sad. He truly liked Daniel. He didn't want to throw Daniel into a den of hungry lions. But the law was the law, and even the king could not change it.

So **faithful** Daniel was thrown into the den of hungry lions. "May your God protect you," said the king as men rolled the stone across the mouth of the den. And King Darius went back to his palace.

But there was no sleep for King Darius that night. He tossed and turned. He turned and tossed. All he could think about was his friend Daniel and those hungry lions. When morning came, the king rushed to where they had left Daniel. "Daniel?" he called out. "Can you hear me?"

Then Daniel called out to the king, "God has sent his angel to shut the lions mouths so that they would not hurt me. O king, I have done no wrong."

Then King Darius wrote to all the peoples who lived within his kingdom, "The God to whom Daniel is **faithful,** is the one and true God. And God's kingdom shall have no end."

Based on Daniel 6.
© 1997 Cokesbury.

Daniel and the Lions Hop
by LeeDell Stickler

Have the children stand in a line, one behind the other. Both hands up like lion's paws. Use these motions (similar to the Bunny Hop) with the chant: hop up and extend right heel out; hop up and bring right foot back into place. Repeat. Do the same on the left foot. Hop forward one hop. Hop backward one hop. Hop forward three hops. Begin the steps over again with each stanza. The teacher should say the first three lines, the children will repeat the fourth line as they hop forward.

O n a land so far away,
There lived a man who liked to pray,
Prayed to God three times a day.
Roar, roar, roar.

Daniel was this faithful man.
He was King Darius' helping hand.
But jealousy soon filled the land.
Roar, roar, roar.

The jealous men dreamed up a plan,
And sent a law throughout the land,
Decreeing prayers to God were banned.
Roar, roar, roar.

But Daniel chose to do what's right
And in his room within plain sight,
He prayed to God both day and night,
Roar, roar, roar.

Daniel was the king's good friend,
But still was put into the den,
Because of other jealous men,
Roar, roar, roar.

With lions Daniel spent the night.
The king rushed down at morning's light
To find that Daniel was all right!
Roar, roar, roar.

Based on Daniel 6.

Where You Go, I Will Go

by LeeDell Stickler

Have the children make a happy face and a sad Face from a paper plate. Let them hold up the appropriate face as the story indicates.

There once was a woman named Naomi. She had a husband and two very fine sons. They lived in the city of Bethlehem. They were very happy. *(Hold up Happy Face.)*

But one day there came a great famine. There was nothing to eat. Naomi and her family had to leave their home and go where there was food to eat. *(Hold up Sad Face.)*

So Naomi and her family moved to Moab. There was plenty of food there. They were very happy. *(Hold up Happy Face.)* But one day, something terrible happened. Naomi's husband became ill and died. Naomi was very sad. How could she go on without her beloved husband? *(Hold up Sad Face.)*

But still Naomi had two wonderful sons. And they took good care of their mother. One day, the sons fell in love and got married. The women were from families who lived in Moab. Naomi loved her new daughters. *(Hold up Happy Face.)*

Then one day something terrible happened. Both of her two sons also died. This left Naomi all alone, except for her two daughters-in-law. *(Hold up Sad Face.)* "I want to go back home," Naomi said to her daughters-in-law, "back to the land where I come from. I have family there who will care for me. You must return to your families. Maybe you can find new husbands." So Naomi set out to go back to her home in Bethlehem. *(Hold up Sad Face.)*

But when Naomi looked back, she saw her two daughters-in-law behind her. "We want to go with you and take care of you," they said. *(Hold up Happy Face.)*

But Naomi told them, "Go back to your families. You have been very kind to me. May the Lord treat you as kindly as you have treated me. But you are too young to be without husbands. Go back." (Hold up Sad Face.)
:
All three women cried, and cried, and cried. And Orpah kissed her mother-in-law and left. But Ruth stayed behind. *(Hold up Happy Face.)* "Do not make me leave you," said Ruth. "Where you go, I will go. Where you live, I will live. Your people shall be my people. Your God will be my God." And Ruth stayed with Naomi. *(Hold up Happy Face.)*

When the two of them came to Bethlehem, the whole town came out to greet them. *(Hold up Happy Face.)* "Is this Naomi who left us so many years ago. We did not recognize you. Where are all your children? Where are their families?" *(Hold up Sad Face.)*

Naomi answered, "Everyone is gone. I am very sad. I have no one." *(Hold up Sad Face.)* But Ruth stayed with her mother-in-law and cared for her. Ruth showed her every kindness. And one day, Ruth married a man named Boaz. Ruth and Boaz had a baby--a grandchild for Naomi to love and care for. *(Hold up Happy Face.)*

Based on Ruth 1-2.

An Esther Melodrama
by LeeDell Stickler

Present this story as an old fashioned melodrama. As each character is introduced into the story, the class and the character will perform these actions:

Esther—Everyone stands up and cheers. Esther waves the queen's traditional wave, palm inward, five fingers extended, waggle the hand back and forth.

Haman—Everyone stands up and boos. Haman twirls imaginary mustache.

Mordecai—Mordecai should grip hands overhead in a traditional victors cheer.

King Ahasuerus—Stands up regally, folds arms across the chest and nods regally.

Assign four children to be the main parts (*Esther, Haman, Mordecai, Ahasuerus*). Everyone will get to cheer or boo as the part indicates. Have the children listen in the story for their character's name. When they hear their name, they stand up and do the indicated action. Caution the children that in real life they would never boo someone. This is just for the fun of telling the story.

Note: If noisemakers are available, let the children use these to make noise each time Haman's name is mentioned.

King Ahasuerus was a very powerful king. One day Queen Vashti made him very angry. She had refused to follow one of his orders. Now, **King Ahasuerus** was not used to having people tell him no. So he decided to get a new queen.

King Ahasuerus held a beauty contest. He invited all the unmarried young women of his kingdom to come before him. From these women, he would choose a new queen.

Mordecai, the palace gatekeeper, had a cousin named **Esther**. **Esther's** parents had died when she was very young and **Mordecai** had raised her as his daughter. Not only was **Esther** beautiful, but she was also kind and loving, and intelligent. "**Esther** would make a wonderful queen," **Mordecai** thought to himself. So, **Mordecai** urged **Esther** to go before the **King Ahasuerus**. But **Mordecai** warned her, "Tell no one of your people. The Jews are not favored in this land. The king may not look upon you kindly if he knows who your people are." And so, **Esther** kept her family a secret.

Esther went to the palace with all the other young women. Finally, **King Ahasuerus** made up his mind. "I choose **Esther** to be my queen. She is very beautiful. She is also kind, loving, and intelligent." He put the crown on her head.

King Ahasuerus had a chief officer named **Haman.** He was proud and cruel. He thought he was very important. So **Haman** made a law: All people will bow down to **Haman.** Everyone was afraid of **Haman.** So, everyone bowed down—everyone except **Mordecai.** This made **Haman** very angry. But **Mordecai** was a Jew. By law, **Mordecai** could bow to no one but God. So **Haman** decided to get rid of **Mordecai** and his people.

Haman came before **King Ahasuerus**, "O Great King, did you know there are people in your land who have their own laws and do not keep your law? You should get rid of them."

King Ahasuerus trusted **Haman**. He did not want these troublesome people in his land. "Do to these people as you will," said the king. **Haman** smiled an evil smile.

When **Mordecai** heard what **Haman** planned to do, he cried out, "Our people are in trouble. Queen **Esther** is our only hope. She must get **King Ahasuerus** to change his mind."

When **Esther** heard what **Mordecai** wanted her to do, she was afraid. "If I go to the king without being called, he will be very angry. He will kill me!"

"Just because you are the Queen does not mean that you will be safe," **Mordecai** cautioned his cousin. "I believe God has a plan for you. Perhaps it was for this reason you became the queen."

Esther knew what she must do. She gathered up her courage and went before **King Ahasuerus**. Instead of being angry, the king was happy to see her. He held out his royal scepter to her. "What do you wish, my queen"

"Please come to a banquet. And bring **Haman** with you," said **Esther**, smiling sweetly.

King Ahasuerus agreed. **Haman** felt even more important than usual.

That night at the banquet, **King Ahasuerus** said, "**Esther**, tell me your wish. I will grant it."

"My king, if you are pleased with me, save my life and the lives of my people!" **Esther** fell to her knees.

"What are you talking about?" **King Ahasuerus** asked. "Who would dare harm my queen and her people?"

"On order went out an order that my people and I are to be killed. Please save us!" **Esther** begged.

"Who ordered such a thing?" the king demanded.

Esther pointed at **Haman**. "This wicked man!" **Haman** knew that he was in deep trouble.

King Ahasuerus jumped up from the table. He paced back and forth trying to decide what to do. Then he ordered: "What **Haman** had planned for you and for all your people shall now be done to him!" Then the king ordered messengers to go throughout the kingdom to undo what he had unknowingly ordered.

So because of Queen **Esther**, the Jewish people were saved. **King Ahasuerus** rewarded **Esther** for her courage and made **Mordecai** his new chief officer. And **Haman** was never heard of again.

Based on the Book of Esther.
© 1997 Abingdon

Psalms

Psalm 15
by LeeDell Stickler

Photocopy this litany. Assign one person to be the Questioner and four other students to be readers. If you have a large class, turn this into a choral reading. Instead of one reader, let that be a group reading. If you have a small group, let children do multiple parts. When it comes to each part, have the child or children stand to respond.

Questioner: Lord, who may enter your Temple? Who may worship on your sacred hill?

Reader 1: A person who obeys God in everything and always does what's right.

Reader 2: A person whose words are true and sincere, who does not say bad things about another person.

Reader 3: A person who is kind to friends

Reader 4: A person who does not spread gossip about neighbors.

Questioner: Lord, who may enter your Temple? Who may worship on your sacred hill?

Reader 1: A person who gives honor to the Lord.

Reader 2: A person who does just as he or she promises, no matter what the cost.

Reader 3: A person who gives without expecting anything in return.

Reader 4: An honest person, one who cannot be bribed to say wrongly about the innocent.

Questioner: Lord, who may enter your Temple? Who may worship on your sacred hill?

All: Whoever does these things will always be secure.

Based on Psalm 15.

A Praise Litany

by LeeDell Stickler

Leader: The Lord is my shepherd; I have everything I need.

All: We thank you, God, for your loving care.

Leader: You let me rest in a soft bed. You let me splash in puddles after the rain.

All: We thank you, God, for your loving care.

Leader: Dear God, you help me feel strong when I feel weak.

All: We thank you, God, for your loving care.

Leader: Even when it is dark, I will not be afraid. I know you are always with me.

All: We thank you, God, for your loving care.

Leader: You give me food to eat, water to drink, and clothes to wear.

All: We thank you, God, for your loving care.

Leader: I know I am safe because you are watching me, guiding me, loving me.

All: We thank you, God, for your loving care.

Based on Psalm 23.

Psalm 8

by Coy Howe

O Lord, your greatness is seen
in all the world!
(Stretch the arms overhead and then hold them out to each side with palms open.)

Your praise reaches up to the heavens.
(Turn the face upward and bring arms above the head.)

You created the moon and the stars.
(Use both hands to make a circle and then make a sweeping motion above the head with one hand.)

You created people like me
to be caretakers of your creation.
(Cross the hands over the chest and turn the head upward.)

O Lord, your greatness is seen
in all the world!
(Stretch the arms overhead and then hold them out to each side with palms open.)

Based on Psalm 8

Psalm 24
by LeeDell Stickler

Teach the children the American Sign Language for the response: The earth belongs to the Lord. Use this for the response where indicated.

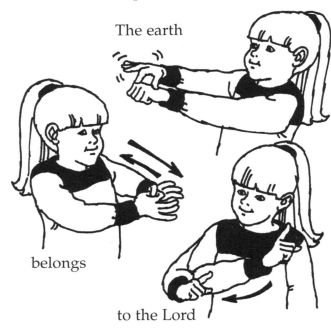

The earth

belongs

to the Lord

Reader 1: The earth and all who live on it are God's.

Reader 2: God built it on the deep waters and laid its foundations in the ocean depths.

Response: *The earth belongs to the Lord.*

Reader 1: Who has the right to go up the Lord's hill?

Reader 2: Those who are pure in act and in thought.

Response: *The earth belongs to the Lord.*

Reader 1: Who may enter God's holy Temple?

Reader 2: Those who do not worship idols or make false promises.

Response: *The earth belongs to the Lord.*

Reader 1: The Lord will bless them and save them.

Reader 2: These are the children of God.

Response: *The earth belongs to the Lord.*

Reader 1: Open wide the gates. Open the ancient doors.

Reader 2: And the great king will come in.

Response: *The earth belongs to the Lord.*

Reader 1: Who is this great king?

Reader 2: It is the Lord, strong and mighty!

Response: *The earth belongs to the Lord.*

Reader 1: Open wide the gates, open the ancient doors.

Reader 2: And the great king will come in.

Response: *The earth belongs to the Lord.*

Reader 1: Who is the great king?

Reader 2: The Lord triumphant!

Based on Psalm 24.

How Majestic Is Your Name

by LeeDell Stickler

Teach the children the movements that correspond with the response. Have the children stand up.

Response:
O LORD *(Stand up. Place palms together, move hands up and apart.)*
How majestic is your name *(Palms facing out, make simultaneous circles with each hand.)*
in all the earth *(Bring arms down, form circle clasping hands in front of body. Sit down.)*

nd God said,
"I will put lights in the sky.
These lights will mark the day and the night.
These lights will show the passing of the months.
These lights will show us when to celebrate special days."

Response:

And God said,
"Let there be a bright light to rule the day.
Let this light shine from morning until evening.
Let this light cause the waters to grow warm.
Let this light cause plants to grow tall.
Let this light cause trees to bear fruit.
Let this light cause flowers to bloom."
And the sun appeared.

Response:

And God said,
"Let there be a softer light to rule the night.
Let this light mark the passing of the days and the months.
Let this light mark the changing of the seasons.
Let there be other lights to keep it company.
Let these lights fill up the nighttime sky."
And the moon and stars appeared.

Response:

And God looked at the sun that God had made.
The sun came up in the morning and set in the evening.
The sun warmed the waters.
The sun caused the plants to grow tall.
The sun caused the trees to bear fruit.
The sun caused the flowers to bloom.
And God was pleased.

Response:

God looked at the moon and the stars.
The moon softly lit the nighttime sky.
The moon marked the passing of the days and the months.
The moon marked the changing of the seasons.
The stars filled the dark night sky.
And God was pleased.

Response:

And God said,
"It is good."
Evening passed and morning came,
Just as God had planned.
That was the fourth day.

Based on Genesis 1:14-19; Psalm 8:1

O Give Thanks to the Lord

by LeeDell Stickler

All: O give thanks to the Lord, for he is good, for his steadfast love endures forever.

Reader 1: For puffy clouds and summer skies, for summer nights and fireflies.

All: O give thanks to the Lord, for he is good, for his steadfast love endures forever.

Reader 2: For leafy trees that give us shade, for watermelon and lemonade.

All: O give thanks to the Lord, for he is good, for his steadfast love endures forever.

Reader 3: For sand castles built upon the beach, and apples that are just out of reach.

All: O give thanks to the Lord, for he is good, for his steadfast love endures forever.

Reader 4: For soft cool grass where we can lay, for fields and yards where we can play.

All: O give thanks to the Lord, for he is good, for his steadfast love endures forever.

Reader 5: For dragonflies that dip and zoom, for summer storms and thunder booms.

All: O give thanks to the Lord, for he is good, for his steadfast love endures forever.

Reader 6: For summertime and all its plea-sures, for summertime with all its treasures.

All: O give thanks to the Lord, for he is good, for his steadfast love endures forever.

Based on Psalm 107.

Psalm 100

by Joyce Brown

Make a joyful noise! *(Lift left hand.)*
X *(Clap right hand against left.)*

Make a joyful noise! *(Lift right hand.)*
X *(Clap left hand against right.)*

Make a joyful noise *(Clap left.)*
for the Lord *(Clap right.)*
our God! *(Thrust arms up and open.)*
Sing a song of love! *(Place left hand at waist, palm up; move right hand making circle.)*
X *(Clap at waist.)*

Sing a song of love! *(Left hand remains at waist, palm up; move right hand making circle.)*
X *(Clap at waist.)*

Sing a song of love *(Clap left.)*
for the Lord *(Clap right.)*
our God! *(Thrust arms up and open.)*
Tell it to the world! *(Turn body full circle left.)*
X *(Clap left.)*
Tell it to the world! *(Turn body full circle right.)*
X *(Clap right.)*
Tell it to the world *(Clap low.)*
for the Lord *(Clap high.)*
our God! *(Thrust arms up and open.)*

Based on Psalm 100.

God's Special Promise

by Gail Britt

Teach the children the sign language for the parenthetical response. Let them practice it several times and watch for your signal to say and sign the words.

Long ago in the country of Judah lived a man named Isaiah. Isaiah was a prophet. God spoke to Isaiah. Isaiah told the people what God said. Isaiah was God's messenger. *(Come, Lord Jesus.)*

At the time Isaiah lived, life was not good for the Hebrew people. The countries around them were fighting with one another. *(Come, Lord Jesus.)* The rich farmers took land away from the poor farmers. *(Come, Lord Jesus.)* The powerful people mistreated the poor people. *(Come, Lord Jesus.)* The people were sad. They cried out to God, "Please send someone to save us!" *(Come, Lord Jesus.)*

God sent a message to the people through Isaiah: A child will be born for you. He will be the leader for God's people. He will be called Savior and Prince of Peace. He will be God's Son. He will be a bright light for those people who are now living in darkness. He will show the people what God is like. He will save them. *(Come, Lord Jesus.)*

How happy the people were to hear Isaiah's words! *(Come, Lord Jesus.)* The people thought, "Life may be bad now, but it will get better. God loves us and cares for us." *(Come, Lord Jesus.)* But the people still had to wait—until the time was right. *(Come, Lord Jesus.)*

Based on Isaiah 9:1-7; 40:1-11.

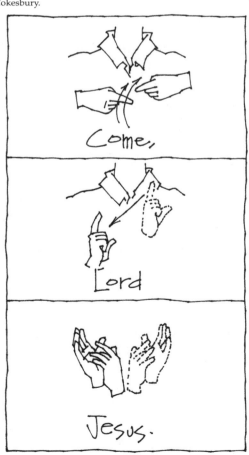

A Special Baby

by Mary Jo Cartledge Hayes

Teach the children the repetitive refrain. Encourage them to say it with you after each stanza.

Going to have a baby.
Going to name him Jesus.
And peace will fill the world.

When Mary was at home
In Nazareth one day,
An angel came to see her.
What did the angel say?

Going to have a baby.
Going to name him Jesus.
And peace will fill the world.

"You are blessed," the angel said.
"The Lord will find a way."
"I'm not afraid," said Mary.
"Let it be just as you say.

Going to have a baby.
Going to name him Jesus.
And peace will fill the world.

Joseph was a carpenter.
He hammered wood all day.
The angel came to visit him.
What did the angel say?

Going to have a baby.
Going to name him Jesus.
And peace will fill the world.

Mary thought about it.
Joseph thought hard, too.
They put their trust in God.
God's love would see them through.

Going to have a baby.
Going to name him Jesus.
And peace will fill the world.

At last God's plan would come to pass.
New hope would fill the earth!
So Mary prayed—and Joseph, too—
As they waited for the birth.

Going to have a baby.
Going to name him Jesus.
And peace will fill the world.

Based on Matthew 1:18-24; Luke 1:26-38.

The Christmas Story

by Judy Gattis Smith

Gather these items:
a leather belt, sandpaper, a rock, a piece of burlap, straw, fake fur, large square of muslin or gauze, plastic star, cotton balls or ball of wool, piece of velvet or silk.
Pass the items around at the indicated time during the story.

Say: Touch and feel the objects as you hear the Christmas story. Think about Mary and Joseph's journey and the stable where Jesus was born.

(Leather belt.)

A long, long time ago Joseph led a donkey. The donkey was carrying Mary on its back. She held tightly to its harness. Mary and Joseph were going to Bethlehem.

(Sandpaper and a rock.)
The road they traveled was dusty, rough, and rocky. It was a long trip and they must have gotten very tired.

(Piece of burlap.)
Mary and Joseph probably carried their belongings in a burlap bag tied to the donkey's back. And when they reached Bethlehem, they probably found the animals' feed stored in burlap sacks in the stable.

(Handful of straw.)
 When Mary laid Jesus in the manger, he probably felt the scratchiness of the hay that lined the manger.

(Piece of fake fur.)
What animals do you think lived in the stable where Jesus was born? Do you think there were sheep, cows, donkeys?

(Large square of muslin or gauze.)
Mary wrapped Jesus in swaddling cloths like all babies born in those days.

(Plastic star or construction paper star.)
We can't feel starlight, but we know a star shone brightly to tell the world that Jesus was born.

(Ball of wool or cotton balls.)
When the shepherds came to see baby Jesus, they brought their sheep with them.

(Piece of velvet or silk.)
Wise men came from the East to see the child Jesus. They brought him gifts to show their love and to rejoice at his birth. The wise men probably wore fine clothes made from fabrics like these.

Based on Luke 2:1-7; Matthew 2:1-12.

Clippity Clop
by Sandra Jimison

As you tell the story, have the children gently slap their legs to make the clippity clop sound.

Mary was so happy. Soon she was going to have a baby! An angel told her she would have a son and name him Jesus.

(Clippity clop! Clippity clop!)

Joseph was happy too. Mary was going to have a baby.

(Clippity clop! Clippity clop!)

Mary and Joseph were going on a trip. They had to go to Bethlehem. The trip from Jerusalem to Bethlehem was a long one. Mary and Joseph had loaded the things they needed on their donkey and were on their way.

(Clippity clop! Clippity clop!)

The donkey traveled along the dirt road. Mary thought about everything the angel had told her. She knew her son would be special. She knew he would teach people how to love one another.

(Clippity clop! Clippity clop!)

Joseph also thought about their special baby. When the baby was born, his name would be Jesus. Joseph knew he and Mary were going to have a special son.

(Clippity clop! Clippity clop!)

Finally, Mary and Joseph entered Bethlehem. Mary knew she would soon give birth to her son.

Based on Luke 1:31, 38, 46-47; 2:1-5.

Good News!

by Sandra Jimison

As you tell the story, have the children clap their hands and make the motions suggested throughout the story. Repeat having the children stomp their feet. Then repeat again having the children stand up and sit down.

Good News! *(Clap, clap.)*
Good News! *(Clap, clap)*
Mary's going to have a baby.
*(Rock arms back and forth
to suggest cradling a baby.)*

Good News! *(Clap, clap.)*
Good News! *(Clap, clap.)*
The baby's name is Jesus.
(Rock arms back and forth.)

Good News! *(Clap, clap.)*
Good News! *(Clap, clap.)*
He will show love to all.
(Hold hands over heart.)

Good News! *(Clap, clap.)*
Good News! *(Clap, clap.)*
He will be called Emmanuel.
(Extend arms out.)

Good News! *(Clap, clap.)*
Good News! *(Clap, clap.)*
He will be the Son of God.
(Extend arms up.)

Good News! *(Clap, clap.)*
Good News! *(Clap, clap.)*
Mary's going to have a baby.
(Rock arms.)

Good News! *(Clap, clap.)*
Good News! *(Clap, clap.)*
The baby's name is Jesus.
(Rock arms.)

Based on Luke 1:26-35; Matthew 1:18-24

Good News Is Coming
by Gail Britt

Teach the children the American sign language for "Good news is coming to you." The story is in the form of a litany. Both voices and hands will help to tell the story. Practice with the children speaking softer and then louder.

Late one night, on a lonely hillside, a group of shepherds watched their sheep. **Shepherds, good news is coming to you.** *(Whisper.)*

The dark night sky was filled with stars. The cold night wind blew and the shepherds huddled together to keep warm. **Shepherds, good news is coming to you.** *(Whisper.)*

Suddenly the sky grew very bright. The stars were pale in comparison. The shepherds were afraid. **Shepherds, good news is coming to you.** *(Normal voice.)*

An angel of the Lord appeared before the shepherds. Great light surrounded the angel. And the shepherds were afraid. **Shepherds, good news is coming to you.** *(Normal voice.)*

"Do not be afraid," the angel said. "I bring you wonderful news. The Savior for whom you have been waiting has been born." **Shepherds, good news is coming to you.** *(Louder voice.)*

"How will we know him?" the shepherds asked. "How will we know it is really him?"

Shepherds, good news is coming to you.

(Louder voice.)

"You will find the baby wrapped in bands of cloth, lying in a manger. And suddenly, there were more angels. Angels filled the sky.

"Glory to God in the highest heaven and peace to all people on earth." **People on earth, good news is coming to you.** *(Shout.)*

When the angels had left, the shepherds said to one another, "Let's go to Bethlehem and find this special baby about whom the angels told us." **People on earth, good news is coming to you.** *(Normal voice.)*

The shepherds found the baby as the angels told them. Then they returned to their flocks, telling everyone they saw of the angels and their message, and the tiny baby in the stable. **People on earth, good news is coming to you.** *(Whisper.)*

Based on Luke 2:8-20

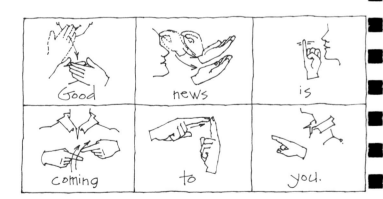

Shepherds on the Hillside
by Raney Good

Add the physical motions as you tell the story.

It was a cold and windy winter night.
The stars were shining clear and bright.
(Hug self as though cold.)

Shepherds sat upon the hill,
The sheep and goats were quiet and still.
(Head on hands as though asleep.)

But suddenly, a light appeared,
And everyone was filled with fear.
(Hands clasped in front of body in fear.)

And unexpectedly that night,
An angel appeared within the light.
(Hand to forehead, look up.)

The angel said, "Good news to all the earth,
I tell you of the Savior's birth.
(Hands in front of body palm up, extended outward.)

You'll find the babe in Bethlehem,
In a manger soft and warm.
(Arms folded as if rocking baby.)

Then angels' singing filled the sky,
"Glory be to God on high.
(Hands to mouth.)

Peace to all,"
The sang so clear,
And then the angels disappeared.
(Look around as if looking for angels.)

Let us find this holy child,
Born on this night so dark and wild.
(Shake finger at one another.)

The shepherds found the peaceful inn,
And stable with the child within.
(Arms folded as if rocking baby.)

They shared with Mary what they had heard,
Related all the angel's words.
(Bend over as if to whisper.)

Then through the town they spread the story,
Of the angel's message and their glory.
(Turn to one another and pretend to talk.)

Praise God for the Savior's birth,
And peace to all upon the earth.
(Hands outstretched overhead, turning around.)

Based on Luke 2:8-20

Jesus Is Born

by LeeDell Stickler

Have the children stand in a circle. The teacher will read the stanzas. Then the children will perform the actions.

In the days of Caesars,
When Augustus wore the crown,
He ordered every citizen
To go to his hometown.
(All children march around circle.)

So, Joseph went to register
With Mary at his side,
The Galilean carpenter
And the girl who'd be his bride.
(Children form pairs and march around circle.)

From the town of Nazareth
The two did make their way,
To the town of Bethlehem,
To find a place to stay.
(Reverse direction and march around circle.)

When Mary and Joseph got to town,
They knocked on every door.
But all the empty spots were filled,
There weren't any more.
(All children knock on pretend door.)

They came upon a little inn,
The light shone bright inside.
The keeper opened up the door,
Joseph stepped aside.
(All children open pretend door.)

"We've no rooms," the keeper said
While standing in the door.
"We don't have a bed at all
No bed, no chair, no floor."
(Cross arms back and forth in front of body.)

But then the keeper looked real close
At the two who stood outside.
The woman's baby was coming soon,
That she couldn't hide.
(Pretend to rock baby.)

"There's a stable out behind the inn,"
The keeper's face grew soft.
"It's warm and safe and dry out there,
And there's hay up in the loft."
(All children sit down on floor.)

That night in the town of Bethlehem,
Within that stable warm,
With all the creatures looking on,
God's only Son was born.
(Rock the baby.)

Based on Luke 2:1-7.

The Birth of Jesus
by Carolyn Stewart

Read the story through one time. Have the children listen carefully. Then read the story a second time and leave out strategic words. Allow the children to fill in the missing words.

Option: Make it a game. Write each of these words on an index card: **Mary, Joseph, stable, baby Jesus, star, sheep, angel, Bethlehem, swaddling clothes, manger, happy, gifts, God.** Hand out the cards to the children. As you read the story, when a child recognizes his or her word, he or she stands up and says it out loud. In a small class, a child might have more than one word. Caution: Make sure each child knows his or her word.

Long ago, a woman named *(Mary)* and a man named *(Joseph)* had to go to Bethlehem to be counted. They could not find a room at the inn, so they stayed in a *(stable)*.

While they were there, something wonderful happened! The wonderful thing was that *(the baby Jesus was born)*. And up in the sky, shining brightly, there was a new *(star)*.

There were some shepherds in the fields watching their *(sheep)*. Suddenly before them was an *(angel)*! They were very much *(afraid)*, for they had not seen an angel before. But the angel said, "Don't be afraid, kind shepherds. I bring you *(good news)* that is for everyone. A baby has been born in *(Bethlehem)*. He is the Savior, the Lord. How will you know him? You will find him wrapped in a *(swaddling clothes)* and lying in a *(manger)*. Many angels now joined the first angel. They sang because they were *(happy)*.

The shepherds hurried to Bethlehem. There they found *(Mary)* and *(Joseph)*, and *(the baby lying in a manger)*. On their way back to the fields, they told everyone they met about the new baby.

There were wise men living in a faraway country. One night they saw a bright, new *(star)*. They searched for the child whose star was in the sky. They followed the star a long time. The star stopped over the house where Jesus lay. The wise men gave Jesus *(gifts)* of gold, frankincense, and myrrh. They worshiped this baby who was the Son of *(God)*.

Based on Luke 2:1-7, Matthew 2:1-12.

Visitors from the East

(A Pantomime Story)

By LeeDell Stickler

Have the children repeat each line after you, imitating your motions. Make the motions large and easy to duplicate.

Once in a land, far, far away
(Point off in the distance.)

There were three wise men
(Index finger to temple as if thinking.)
Who studied the stars.
(Pretend to use a telescope.)

One night they saw a brand new star—
(Point up and jump up and down in excitement.)
The sign that a new king had been born.
(Pretend to place crown on head.)

"We must go and find this wonderful thing,"
(Hold arms as if rocking a tiny baby.)
they said, and set off on their camels
(Hold pretend reins, bend and straighten knees.)
Following the wondrous star.
(Point to the sky, continue riding camel.)

They went over tall, tall, hills.
(Stand on tip toe and ride camels.)
They rode through dry, dry deserts,
(Ride camel and grab throat.)
Following the wondrous star.
(Point to sky, continue riding camel.)

Finally, they came to the city of Jerusalem
(Pull back on reins and bring camel to halt.)
They asked every one they saw.

(Turn to the right and left with hand to mouth.)
Have you heard about the new king?
(Place a pretend crown on the head.)
But no one knew what they were talking about.
(Shake head sadly.)

King Herod heard about the three strange men.
(Hand cupped to ear.)
He called them to come before him.
(Bow low before the king.)
"Why are you here?" he asked them
(Hands extended in question.)
"We've come to see the baby,"they said
(Pretend to rock the baby.)
"The one whohas been born to be king.
(Place pretend crown on head.)
Do you know where he is?"
(Hold arms out in question.)

Now King Herod was quite upset.
(Cross arms over chest. Tap foot angrily.)
He called together all his best advisors.
(Hands to mouth as if calling out.)
"What's the meaning of all of this?" he asked.
(Cross arms over chest. Tap foot angrily.)
The Scriptures say a baby will be born
(Pretend to rock baby.)
In the tiny town of Bethlehem.
(Point to the left or right.)
The baby will grow to be a king.
(Pretend to place crown on the head.)

This did not make the king happy.
(Cross arms over chest. Look angry.)
But King Herod sent the wise men on their way.
(Wave goodbye.)
"When you find the baby,"
(Pretend to rock the baby.)
Tell me where he is.
(Point to self.)
I would like to visit him too."
(Clasp hands in front of body, looking sincere.)

And so the wise men left the city.
(Pretend to ride a camel.)
The star led them to a small house
(Point to the sky.)
Where they found the child Jesus.
(Pretend to rock the baby.)
And they bowed down to him
(Kneel down.)
And gave him gifts of gold, frankincense, and myrrh.
(Hold out arms as if presenting gifts.)
Then they returned to their country

(Pretend to ride camel to the right.)
By another route.
(Make a quick turn and ride camel to the left.)

Based on Matthew 2:1-12.

Extending the story: Use the star pattern here to create a Star Parade. Each child will need two. Color and cover with glitter. Glue on either side of a wooden dowel. Have the children parade through the church singing "We Three Kings of Orient Are." At every place they stop, let them ask: We are looking for the newborn king. Have you seen him?

Followers of Jesus

Jesus Calls Disciples
by Sharilyn S. Adair

Have the children repeat the actions and the last sentence you say.

Jesus was standing on the lakeshore teaching. Lots and lots of people came to hear him. Then more came. And more. Oh, my! How could they all see and hear him? *(Hands to sides of face in surprise.)*
(Children: *How could they all see and hear him?*)

Jesus had an idea. Simon the fisherman and his partners were washing their nets on the shore. "Come here, Simon," said Jesus. *(Motion with right hand to come.)*
(Children: *"Come here, Simon," said Jesus.*)

"Will you take me out in your boat so that people can see me from the shore?"
"Yes, I will," said Simon. *(Nod head.)*
(Children: *"Yes, I will," said Simon.*)

And he did. Now all the people could see and hear Jesus. When Jesus finished talking to the people, he said to Simon, "Row out to deeper water and put your nets down for some fish. *(Make rowing motion with hands and arms.)*
(Children: *"Put your nets down for some fish."*)

"Fish!" said Simon. "There aren't any fish. We've been fishing all night without catching fish. But if you say so, I will let down the nets." *(Throw both arms out as if casting a net.)*
(Children: *"If you say so, I will let down the nets."*)

And he did. Simon began to pull the nets in again. The nets were heavy. He tugged and tugged. "Fish!" cried Simon. "I never saw so many fish!" *(Act as though pulling on a very heavy net.)*
(Children: *"Fish!" cried Simon. "I never saw so many fish!"*)

Simon needed help. He called to his partners, "Bring another boat. There are too many fish." *(Motion with right hand to come.)*
(Children: *"Bring another boat. There are too many fish."*)

James and John came to help. They piled up fish until both boats were full. The fishermen were amazed. "We have never seen this many fish before," they said. *(Hold both hands and arms out and up in amazement.)*
(Children: *"We have never seen this many fish before," they said.*)

Jesus smiled at them. "Do not be afraid," he said, "from now on you will be catching people." *(Reach out first with right hand and bring into the body. Reach out with left hand and bring into the body.)*
(Children: "From now on you will be catching people.")

The fishermen rowed the boats to shore. Then they left their boats and followed Jesus. *(Wave goodbye to boats.)*
(Children: "They left their boats and followed Jesus.")

Based on Luke 5:1-11.

Clink, Clink, Clink
by LeeDell Stickler

Give each child a handful of pennies or metal washers. Provide a large coffee can or other aluminum can. When you come to the response part of the story, let the children drop their coins into the can, one at a time. Drop them from a height so that they will make noise as they fall.

Response:
Clink, clink, clink
A tax collector he
When Jesus said to Matthew
"Please, come follow me."

Once there was a tax collector. His name was Matthew. Some people called him Levi. Every day he sat in his office collecting taxes from the people.

Response:

Matthew collected taxes for the Romans. The people of Palestine did not like the Romans. They did not like tax collectors. So they did not like Matthew.

Response:

The people left Matthew out of all their activities. They did not invite Matthew to join them for dinner. They did not invite Matthew to spend time and talk with them.

Response:

One day Jesus appeared in the market place. He saw Matthew sitting in his office collecting taxes. Jesus came up to him and said, "Follow me."

Response:

Matthew invited Jesus to come to his house. He invited other tax collectors to join them. Some Pharisees saw this and asked: Why does Jesus eat with such people?

Response:

And Jesus said, "People who are well do not need a doctor. I have come to call the outcasts and the sinners."

Response:
Based on Matthew 9:9-13, Luke 5:27-32

Jesus Sends Out The Disciples

by LeeDell Stickler

When the children come to the refrain, let them link arms with a partner and skip around in a circle as they say the refrain. Let them practice several times before you beginn the story. Children must change partners for every refrain.

Refrain:
Two by two, two by two,
Jesus sent them two by two.

Jesus told his friends one day,
"I've a task for you to do.
Go throughout the countryside,
Go out two by two."

Refrain:
Two by two, two by two,
Jesus sent them two by two.

"Take nothing with you on your trip,
But the clothes that you now wear.
No food, no bag, no money,
You can travel without a care."

Refrain:
Two by two, two by two,
Jesus sent them two by two.

"The places where you are going
Should give you all you need,
Be my witness in all you do,
In thought, in word, and deed."

Refrain:
Two by two, two by two,
Jesus sent them two by two.

"You will talk to people
My message you will teach.
Tell them all about God's love,
About God's kingdom preach."

Refrain:
Two by two, two by two,
Jesus sent them two by two.

"Go to every village,
In just one place you'll stay.
If no one there will welcome you,
Then simply go away."

Refrain:
Two by two, two by two,
Jesus sent them two by two.

And so, they all went on their way
They traveled up and down.
They preached the good news everywhere,
In villages and towns.

Refrain:
Two by two, two by two,
Jesus sent them two by two.

Jesus is God's only Son,
We celebrate his birth.
Jesus taught about God's love,
God's love for all the earth.

Refrain:
Two by two, two by two,
Jesus sent them two by two.

Based on Mark 6:6-13, 30-32.

Calling The Twelve
by LeeDell Stickler

Have the children repeat each line after you.

Peter, Andrew, James and John,
Drop your nets and come along.

Levi, Philip, Bartholomew
I've got important work for you.

James the son of Alphaeus
And Thomas, will you join with us?

Thaddaeus and Judas too,
Don't you know, I'm calling you.

Simon the Zealot, lend a hand.
Won't you join our merry band?

Disciples twelve, now you will see,
I'm calling you to follow me.

Based on Mark 1:16-20;
2:13-17; 3:13-19.

Play a Clapping Game
by LeeDell Sticklerr

Arrange the children in pairs facing one another. Children will play a clapping game as they learn the rhyme. Repeat the poem with them until they learn it easily.

Children will pat their lap with both hands, clap hands together, pat hands together in the center, clap hands, pat their lap again. Repeat three more times with a slight variation on the last pat. On the last pat, the children will reach up high and pat each other's hands.

Christians (*Pat knees with both hands.*) follow (*Clap hands.*) Jesus. (*Pat each other's hands, clap hands.*)

Christians (*Pat knees.*) love (*Clap hands.*) the Lord. (*Pat each other's hands, clap.*)

Christians (*Pat knees.*) love (*Clap hands.*) one another (*Pat each other's hands, clap.*) and show it (*Pat knees.*) more (*Clap hands.*) and more. (*Pat each other's hands, reaching up high.*)

Looking For Disciples
by Sue Downing

The children will repeat each line after the leader and do the actions.

Let's look for disciples
Let's walk with Jesus.
We want to go,
Yes!
(Tap hands on thighs like walking.)

Let's put on sandals,
(Pretend to slip feet into sandals.)
Take a walking stick,
(Reach arm out for a walking stick.)
and pack some food.
(Put food in a pouch.)
Here we go!

We're going to look for disciples.
(Place hand above eyes and look all around.)
Up and down hillsides,
(Move hands up and back down.)
past swaying trees,
(Hold arms and sway back and forth.)
through desert sand.
(Tap hands on thighs slowly.)

Look! We've come to the Sea of Galilee.
(Place hand on forehead and look around.)
We see some fishermen.
(Make motion like throwing out fishing net.)
Come follow Jesus!
(Beckon with hand.)
They want to go.
Yes!

Jesus looks at us.
(Place hand on forehead and look around.)
"Will you follow me?" Jesus asks.
What do we answer?
"Yes!"
(Nod head yes!)

Based on Luke 5:1-11.

Blind Bartimaeus
by Sue Downing

Children will do the actions after each section of the poem.

On Bible times very long ago,
Jesus traveled to a city called Jericho.
*(Walk in place or walk
around in your circle.)*

There by the roadside
sat a man who couldn't see.
*(Sit down on the floor and
put hands over your eyes.)*

When Jesus came by he shouted,
"Lord, have mercy on me!"
*(Cup hands around mouth
and shout together the words
Bartimaeus says.)*

"Be quiet," many said to the
poor, blind man.
(Hold fingers up to lips.)

But Bartimaeus replied, "I'll
shout as loud as I can!"
*(Cup hands around mouth
and shout together the words
Bartimaeus says.)*

Jesus then said to Bartimaeus,
"This is what you must do."
*(Point index finger and move
up and down.)*

"Take heart, get up, I'm
calling for you!"
*(Move arm as if motioning
someone to come.)*

So Bartimaeus threw off his
coat,
(Move arms outward.)
sprang up and came
*(Jump up and move legs up
and down.)*
And said, "Teacher, please let
me see again!"
(Fold hands in prayer.)

Jesus said to him, "Go, your
faith has made you well."
(Point arm outward.)

"Wow! What a story
Bartimaeus had to tell!"
*(Have the children repeat this
line after you.)*

Based on Mark 10:46-52.

Friends In Deed
by LeeDell Stickler

Select four children to be the four friends who carried the parlytic to see Jesus. At a certain cue, let them stand up and repeat the response. If you have a small group, write the response on a piece of posterboard and let the whole group read it at a certain cue.

Response:
Oh, Jesus, Jesus, we have heard
(Put hand to ear.)
That you can heal with a single word.
(Fingers touch lips and hand comes down, palm up.)
It wouldn't take so very much,
(Both hands extended, palms up.)
For we've a friend who needs your touch.
(Both hands extended, palms down.)

Wherever Jesus went, people followed. They had heard about all the wonderful things Jesus did. They had heard about all the wonderful things Jesus said. They wanted to see and hear these things for themselves.

Response: *(Four friends stand up; repeat poem.)*

Because the crowd was so large, Jesus began teaching outdoors. There were few houses that would hold so many people. And everyone wanted to see and hear Jesus.

Response: *(Four friends stand up; repeat poem.)*

One day Jesus was visiting friends in Capernaum. The news soon spread that Jesus was in town. People came from nearby villages and towns. In the crowd were Pharisees and teachers of the Law Who wanted to learn more about this man Jesus.

Response: *(Four friends stand up; repeat poem.)*

People crowded into the small house where Jesus was staying. Some people brought with them persons who were sick or disabled. They wanted Jesus to make their friends well.

In the town were four men. They had a friend who could not move. The doctors had not been able to make their friend well. Maybe Jesus could.

Response: *(Four friends stand up; repeat poem.)*

The four men put their friend on a pallet and carried him to where Jesus was teaching. But when they got there they found a huge crowd of people. There were so many people that they could not get into the house at all.

Response: *(Four friends stand up; repeat poem.)*

Suddenly, one of the men said, "I know how we can get inside." Up to the roof of the house they went, carrying their friend. Carefully, carefully, the men removed sections of the roof. Soon there was a hole—a hole just big enough for their friend's bed.

The men tied ropes to their friend's bed. They lowered him slowly through the hole in the roof. Down, down, down the man went. When the pallet came to a stop, the man was hanging right in front of Jesus.

Response: *(Four friends stand up; repeat poem.)*

Jesus looked at the man on the bed. He looked up at the man's friends on the roof. These men believed that Jesus could make their friend well.

"Friend," Jesus said, "your sins are forgiven." The Pharisees and teachers of the Law gasped.

"Who was this man?"

But Jesus said, "Would it be easier for me to say, 'Stand up and walk?' Either way you will know that I speak with the power of God." Jesus looked at the man on the pallet. "Take up your bed and walk."

The man stood up, took his bed, and went to his home praising God. And everyone who saw what happened was amazed.

Response: *(Four friends stand up; repeat poem.)*

Based on Luke 5:17-26.

Jesus and Zacchaeus
by Sharilyn S. Adair

Characters

Narrator
Bystander 1
Bystander 2
Zacchaeus
Jesus

Narrator: The streets of Jericho are crowded. All through the town people are coming out of their shops and houses to see what is happening. Many of them are talking excitedly with one another.

Bystander 1: Have you heard the news? Jesus is coming through our town today. I've never seen him, have you?

Bystander 2: No, but I certainly want to see him. I've heard a lot about him. My neighbor Jonathan saw him heal a paralyzed man once. Can you imagine that? And they say he's very wise. Even the Pharisees ask him questions.

Zacchaeus: Excuse me! Excuse me! Can I get through? I can't see from back here.

Bystander 2: Go away, Little Man! We were here first. Find your own place to watch for Jesus.

Zacchaeus: Oh! I get the same story everywhere. Nobody likes me. Well, I'll show them the next time they come to me to pay their taxes! They'll wish they had been nicer to me when they find out how much I'm going to charge them. Goodness, at this rate I'll never get to see Jesus. There are too many people in the way, and they're all taller than I am. I know! I'll climb that sycamore tree. There's a good-sized limb hanging over the road. From there I should be able to see everything;

Bystander 1: Here he comes! Here comes Jesus! Look! He's stopping right under that sycamore tree.

Jesus: Zacchaeus, hurry and come down; for I must stay at your house today.

Bystander 2: Did you hear what he said? Did he really say what I think he said? I can't believe my ears!

Bystander 1: Zacchaeus! He's going to stay with Zacchaeus? Everyone knows what a sinner Zacchaeus is. Why, he's probably stolen from half the people in town. Doesn't Jesus know that?

Narrator: It's later now. Earlier today Zacchaeus welcomed Jesus into his home. After a meal and a long talk with Jesus, Zacchaeus seems to be a changed person.

Zacchaeus: Half of my possessions, Lord, I will give to the poor. And if I have cheated anyone of anything, I will pay back four times as much.

Jesus: Good for you, Zacchaeus. Today salvation has come to this house.

Based on Luke 19:1-9.

From *Don't Just Sit There: Bible Stories That Move You For Ages 3-5.*
© 1997 by Abingdon Press. Reprinted by Permission.

Five Loaves and Two Fish
by Sue Downing

Jesus and his disciples
Were traveling one day,
When they heard the sound of footsteps
Slowly coming their way.
(Make footstep sounds.)

So they turned and looked behind them,
And what did they see?
(Turn head around.)
A large crowd of people
(Stretch arms to the side.)
Near the Sea of Galilee.
(Make wave motions with hands.)

Jesus said, "I'm tired and hungry,
And I know this crowd is too!"
(Pat stomach.)
The disciples shook their heads saying,
"What are we going to do?"
(Shake heads from side to side.)

"There's not enough money
To buy so much bread.
I see a boy with some bread and fish,"
(Point.)
One of Jesus' disciples said.

So Jesus asked the little boy
In a very kind way,
"Will you please share your food
With these hungry folk today?"

The boy gladly gave Jesus
His basket of fish and bread.

(Extend hands outward.)
And the food was passed out
Until 5,000 were fed!
(Pretend to eat.)

"This is a miracle!"
All the people cried.
Five barley loaves and two small fish
You've greatly multiplied!

We never will forget
What you, Jesus, have done.
(Shake head no.)
Surely, it is true.
You must be God's only Son."
(Kneel and fold hands in prayer.)

Based on John 6:1-15.
© 1996 Cokesbury

Parables and Teachings

The Good Samaritan
by Nancy Holbrook Sweeney

Children will add sound effects of the various characters by using their voices, their hands, and their feet.

A traveler: *Whistle happily.*
The robbers: *Slap thighs quietly and rapidly several times to make running sound.*
The priest: *Snap fingers.*
The Levite: *Stomp feet loudly.*
The Good Samaritan and his donkey: *Make clicking noise with tongue.*

Say: When a lawyer asked Jesus, "Who is my neighbor?" Jesus answered by telling a story.

A **traveler** was walking along a dusty road from Jerusalem to Jericho.
He was tired and walked slowly.
The **traveler** led a donkey, loaded with things to sell at the marketplace.

Suddenly a group of **robbers** jumped out of some bushes by the road.
They beat the **traveler.**
They took away his donkey and goods.
The **robbers** ran away and left **traveler** there for dead.

The **traveler** lay hurt by the side of the road. He wondered if anyone would come by and help him.

A **priest** was going down that road.
He saw the injured **traveler**.
"Should he help?" he asked himself.
He knew he should.
But if he did, he'd be late to the Temple.
It wouldn't do for a **priest** to be late!
So, he passed by on the other side of the road.

A **Levite** came down the road. He was a priest's helper.
From far away he too saw the **traveler** lying ont he side of the road.
He was afraid to help.
He thought the **robbers** might still be near and might hurt him too.
The **Levite** walked a little faster and went on by.
Then a **Samaritan** came by on his donkey.
He saw the **traveler** lying on the side of the road.

The **Samaritan** didn't think about who the **traveler** was.
The **Samaritan** didn't think about what else he had to do that day.
All the **Samaritan** saw was someone who needed help.
The **Samaritan** poured oil on the **traveler's** wounds.
He bound them up with cloth.
He gave the **traveler** water.
Then he put the man on his donkey.

The **Samaritan** took the injured **traveler** to the nearest inn.
He paid the innkeeper money to take care of the man.
He told the innkeeper, "Care for him and if I owe you more money, when I pass this way again, I will pay you."

And Jesus asked: Who was the good neighbor?

Based on Luke 10:25-37.

The Unforgiving Servant
by Julie Kuhn Wallace

Have the children perform these actions every time they hear those particular words:

King: *Act as though putting a crown on the head.*

Money: *Right hand pretends to place coins in the left hand palm.*

Servant: *Hands clasped in front, bow from the waist.*

Once there was a powerful **king** who wished to settle accounts with his servants who had borrowed **money.**

One man owed the **king** a lot of **money**—more than ten thousand talents. The **king** had him brought to the palace and asked him to pay the **money** he owed.

"My **king**, I cannot pay you your **money**," the **servant** said. "I do not have it!"

The **king** replied, "Then I will have to sell you, your wife, and your children to make payment."

The **servant** fell on his knees and begged, "Please, my **king**, be patient and give me more time. I will give you the **money** I owe you—I promise!"

The **king** felt sorry for the man. "I will forget your debt," the **king** said. "You may go free."

On his way out, the **servant** met a man who owed him some **money,** about one day's wage. "Pay me the **money** you owe now!" the **servant** insisted.

This man also pleaded. "Have patience with me. I will pay you all the **money** I owe."

No way," said the **servant**. "I will have you thrown in jail until you give me my **money**."

When the **king** heard about his **servant's** unforgiving actions, he called for him. "I can't believe you didn't forgive that man who owed you **money!** Did you forget that I had forgiven you?"

In anger, the **king** had the **servant** thrown into jail.

Based on Matthew 18:23-34.

Welcome Home

by Julia Kuhn Wallace

Children will add the sound effects to the following story. Prepare signal cards as shown here. Hold up each card as indicated in the story and let the children make the appropriate sounds.

Signal Cards:
Applause
What?
Oh, no!
Sigh!
Hurray!
Boo!

There was a man who had two sons. *(Applause.)*

One day, the younger son said, "Father, give me my share of your property now." *(What?)*

The father was not pleased, but he did as he was asked. He divided his property between the two sons. *(Sigh!)*

The young son left home and traveled far away where he spent his money recklessly. *(Oh, no!)*

When a famine came, he was hungry. *(Sigh!)*
So that he would have food to eat, the son took a job feeding pigs. In fact, he was so hungry that he would have gladly eaten what the pigs were fed. *(Oh, no!)*

After a time, he thought of his father. *My father's workers eat better than I do!* he thought. *I will go home to my father and apologize. Maybe he will hire me to work. Then I will be able to eat.* *(Sigh!)*

A few days later the father looked down the road and saw his younger son returning home. *(Hurray!)*
He ran to his son to welcome him home. *(Applause.)*

"Father," said the son, "I'm sorry. I have sinned against God and you. Please take me back as one of your workers." *(Applause.)*

But instead of hiring his son to work in the fields, the father planned a big party to celebrate his son's homecoming. The father loved his son and forgave him for all the mistakes he had made. *(Hurray!)*

When the older son saw that his brother had returned home, he was angry. *(What?)*

"My father never gave me a party. And I was a good son. I stayed home and worked hard." *(Sigh!)*

"It's not fair," he said. *(Boo!)*

"But my son, you are always with me," the father said. "Everything I have is yours. Now, we must celebrate—for your brother who was as good as dead to us is now alive. He is no longer lost, but has been found."*(Hurray!)*

Based on Luke 15:11-32.

The Lost Sheep

by LeeDell Stickler

Children will pretend to be the flock of sheep. They will follow the actions as indicated by the teacher and respond Baa at the end of each verse.

Make costumes by attaching ears to a circular band. Make a set of ears for each child.

Once there was a shepherd
    who had one hundred sheep.
He found cool water for them to drink
    and green grass for them to eat.
(If you have room, walk about and gesture to the floor for the grass and water.)

Response: ("Baa, baa.")

He cared for all his sheep
    and kept them safe from harm.
He built a pen of sticks and stones
    to keep them dry and warm.
(Bring the sheep together into a group.)

Response: ("Baa, baa.")
"Come, little sheep," the shepherd called,
    "Let's go out for the day."
The sun is warm and the grass is fresh.
    You can run and play."
(Lead the sheep out of the fold.)

Response: ("Baa, baa.")

And when the sun begins to set
    and the sky's no longer light,
We'll come back down the mountainside,
    together for the night."
(Bring the sheep back to the fold.)

Response: ("Baa, baa.")

One, two, three, four, five and six,
    seven, eight and nine,
The shepherd counted every one
    till he got to ninety-nine.
(Count the children as they pass before you.)

Response: *("Baa, baa.")*

I must have counted wrong, he said,
    and counted them again,
But all he found were ninety-nine sheep,
    standing in the pen.
(Count the children again.)

Response: *("Baa, baa.")*

"There were one hundred sheep this morning!"
    he cried in great distress.
"If one is missing from the flock,
    I'll be in such a mess."
(Teacher puts hands over face and looks distressed.)

Response: *("Baa, baa.")*

The shepherd left the ninety-nine
    to search for the one lost sheep,
He had to find the missing one,
    before he went to sleep.
(Shepherd leaves the group and looks for the lost one.)

Response: *("Baa, baa.")*

"He could have fallen off the cliff
    or been eaten by a bear.
He could have fallen in the stream
    and drowned with me not there."
(Look over pretend cliff.)

Response: *("Baa, baa.")*

"There you are!" the shepherd said,
    when the one lost sheep he spied,
"Don't move a muscle or you'll fall,"
    the frightened shepherd cried.
(Shepherd points, looking frightened.)

Response: *("Baa, baa.")*

He scooped the missing sheep right up

into his waiting arms.
"I'll take you home," the shepherd said,
    "back where it's safe and warm."
(Shepherd picks up pretend sheep and snuggles it against him/her or hugs child who was the lost sheep.)

Response: *("Baa, baa.")*

"Let's celebrate," the shepherd said,
    "I've found my little lost sheep.
And now that all are home again,
    I know that I can sleep."
(Jump up and down in celebration.)

Response: *("Baa, baa.")*

When Jesus told this story,
    to people long ago,
He wanted them to know that
    God does love them so.
(Hug self.)

Based on Luke 15:1-7.

Lost and Found
by Julie Kuhn Wallace

Prepare a piece of paper as shown here. Take a pair of scissors. Make the cuts in the paper as the story indicates.

Once there was a shepherd who had one hundred sheep! That's a lot of sheep to take care of. But the shepherd did it! The shepherd made sure each one had food and water and was safe from wild animals. Do you have anything that is so important that you take care of it like the shepherd takes care of the sheep?

Every night, before the shepherd went to sleep, he gathered his flock and counted each sheep. Ninety-seven, ninety-eight, ninety-nine . . . Uh-Oh! He thought to himself. Then he counted again. Only ninety-nine sheep! One was missing!
(Fold a paper in half lengthwise.)

The shepherd climbed over a steep hill and looked. No sheep!
(Cut from A to B.)

He went down into a rocky valley and looked around. No sheep!
(Cut from B to C.)

He looked in the thorn bushes! No sheep!
(Cut from C to D.)

He even looked by the river where they had gone earlier for water. Still no sheep!
(Cut from D to E.)

He wasn't going to give up. The shepherd would look everywhere—no matter how long it took—until he found his lost sheep.

Suddenly, he heard a "Baa." The lost sheep was caught in a bush behind a big rock where the shepherd could hardly see. The shepherd ran over to pick up the sheep. He checked to be sure the sheep was not hurt. Then he carried the tired sheep all the way back to the sheepfold where the other sheep were already beginning to go to sleep.

The shepherd already had ninety-nine sheep safe in the sheepfold. Why did he take so much time to look for his one lost sheep?
(Cut from E to F. Then, unfold the paper. Show the children the heart shape.)

Jesus told this story about the way the shepherd loves his sheep to remind us that God loves each one of us that much too. Isn't it wonderful to know that God cares for us?

Based on Matthew 18:12-14.

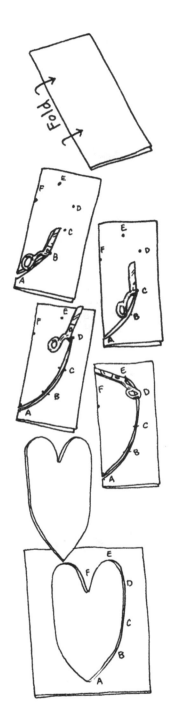

A Special Teacher
by Julia Kuhn Wallace

Narrator 1: After Jesus began to teach in the synagogues, he returned to Nazareth in Galilee, where he had grown up. On the Sabbath he went to the synagogue as was his custom.

Narrator 2: At the synagogue an attendant handed him a scroll from the prophet Isaiah and invited him to read to the people who were gathered there. Jesus took the scroll, stood up, and began to read.

Group 1: "The Spirit of the Lord is upon me,

Group 2: because he has anointed me to bring good news to the poor.

Group 1: He has sent me to proclaim release to the captives

Group 2: and recovery of sight to the blind,

Group 1: to let the oppressed go free,

Group 2: to proclaim the year of the Lord's favor."

Narrator 2: When Jesus had finished reading, he rolled up the scroll, returned it to the attendant, and sat down.

Narrator 1: Everyone looked at Jesus in amazement when he said, "Today, this scripture has been fulfilled in your hearing."

Based on Luke 4:14-22.

© 1995 Cokesbury.

Cock-a doodle-doo!
by LeeDell Stickler

Let the children make rooster puppets from lunch-sized paper bags as shown here. The children can use the puppets to be roosters and crow the refrain.

Refrain:
Cock-a doodle-doodle,
Cock-a doodle-do!
Peter broke his promise.
Now what will he do?

To the garden the soldiers rushed
With swords and spears held high.
All the others ran away,
But Peter stayed close by.
They led their prisoner down the street.
His hands and feet were bound.
They brought him to the high priest's house;
The council gathered 'round.

Refrain:
Cock-a doodle-doodle, Cock-a doodle-do!
Peter broke his promise.
Now what will he do?

"You say you are the Son of God,
The Son of God Most High!"
Jesus said, "That's what you say."
"We've heard him!" the people lied.
Peter stood outside the house,
For he was Jesus' friend,
He wondered what would happen
When the trial came to an end.

Refrain:
Cock-a doodle-doodle, Cock-a doodle-do!
Peter broke his promise.
Now what will he do?

A serving girl saw Peter.
The fire lit up his face.
"You look like someone I have seen,
But in some other place."
I think you are the prisoner's friend,"
And Peter turned away.
"I do not know of whom you speak.
"You are wrong in what you say!"

Refrain:
Cock-a doodle-doodle, Cock-a doodle-do!
Peter broke his promise.
Now what will he do?

"I believe the girl is right.
Your voice gives you away!"
"You sound like him," another said.
"Don't turn your face away!"
"I do not know him!" Peter cried
And moved away from them.
"You are mistaken in what you say.
I really DO NOT KNOW HIM!"

Refrain:
Cock-a doodle-doodle, Cock-a doodle-do!
Peter broke his promise.
Now what will he do?

The sky was getting lighter.
The day would soon be here.
A rooster climbed upon the wall,
And sang out loud and clear.
When Peter heard the rooster,
He thought his heart would break.
Those words "I do not know him!"
Meant he'd broke the vow he'd made.

Based on Mark 14:26-31, 66-72.

Jesus Comes to Jerusalem
(An Echo Pantomime)
by Mary Jane Pierce-Norton

Read the words and do the actions. Instruct the children to repeat your actions.

I was a child in Jesus' day.
(Stand straight.)
One day I put on my sandals.
(Slip on sandals.)
And put on my robe.
(Slip arm into cloak.)
And hurried past the city gate.
(Run in place.)
I was very happy and excited.
(Jump up and down.)
I called my friends to join me.
(Beckon with arm.)
I told them Jesus was coming.
(Whisper together.)
We walked on together.
(Walk in place.)
We looked to see if he was coming.
(Shade eyes.)
But we saw nothing.
(Shake head "no.")
It was hard to wait.
(Shift feet.)
Then we saw him.
(Point.)
We left our parents and ran.
(Run in place.)
He was riding a donkey.
(Slap one thigh, then the other. Clap and repeat.)

Let's get some branches and
(Reach up.)
wave them.
(Wave.)
"Hosanna, Hosanna!"
(Continue waving.)
We are heading down the
(Donkey claps.)
path past Gethsemane now.
Now we're going across the Kidron Valley.
(Continue donkey claps.)
My father is throwing down his cloak
(Point.)
I want to, too.
(Slip out of cloak. Spread it on the ground.)
Hey, wait for me.
(Grab up cloak.)
We're going into the walled
(Snap fingers.)
city of Jerusalem now.
The crowd is too big.
(Stand on tiptoes.)
They are shouting too loud.
(Cover ears.)
We are being pushed to the back.
(Pantomime being pushed back.)
Look, Jesus is turning around
(Wave back.)
and waving goodby to us.
"Goodby, Jesus. Goodby."
(Repeat words.)

Based on Matthew 21:6-11.

Hosanna!
by LeeDell Stickler

Let the children make paper figures to represent the crowd that greeted Jesus when he came to Jerusalem. Attach each figure to a wooden craft stick, a plastic drinking straw, or an unsharpened pencil.

Say: Pretend you are the crowd that greeted Jesus on the day he came to Jerusalem. When it comes your part of the story, stand up and wave the figures and say:

Hosanna! Hosanna!
He comes in the name of the Lord.

It was springtime in Palestine and the time of Passover was near. People from the villages and towns filled the roads. Men, women, children talked and sang as they made their way to the great city of Jerusalem. Passover was a time to celebrate freedom. Soon the roads were filled to overflowing. *(Refrain.)*

Jesus and his friends were among those people traveling to Jerusalem. It was a long trip and until now they had been traveling on foot. Jesus sent his friends to the next village to get him a donkey to ride on. It was a small gray donkey, and Jesus' friends put their cloaks on its back. *(Refrain.)*

Once again they set off down the road. "Good day" and "How is your family?" Good neighbors greeted one another. Some were neighbors of Jesus and his friends. When they recognized Jesus, they began to whisper to one another. "Jesus is coming to Jerusalem for the Passover." *(Refrain.)*

Some people asked, "Who is this Jesus you are talking about?"
"It's Jesus the teacher. Jesus the healer. It's Jesus the prophet from Nazareth," they answered. But some said, "It is Jesus, the Son of God. And he is coming to Jerusalem for the Passover." *(Refrain.)*

As the word spread along the road, people began to stop and wait and watch. Some cut palm branches from the trees and waved them as Jesus passed. Some laid their cloaks down on the road for the little donkey to walk on. As Jesus passed by they shouted, "Blessed is the one who comes in the name of the Lord."*(Refrain.)*

Based on Mark 11:1-10.

An Easter Story

by LeeDell Stickler

Using the pattern provided, make butterfly puppets for each child. If you have time,, children can decorate their own puppets. The puppet will fit on their right (or left) index finger. Children will wave their puppet up and down at the appropriate places in the story.

Say: We use the butterfly as a symbol for Jesus' death and resurrection. The butterfly begins life as a tiny egg. The egg hatches into a caterpillar. The caterpillar eats and eats and eats until the time is ready. Then it spins a coccoon and sleeps. While the caterpillar sleeps marvelous things happen to its body. It changes into a completely different creature. When we believe in Jesus, then we become like the butterfly, new and different creatures, too.

Refrain:
Butterflies of every color.
Fluttering on their way
Remind us all that Jesus lives
On this Easter day!

Have you heard the good news? Jesus is not dead! He is alive! You may not believe it. But I can promise you it is true. Jesus is alive.

Refrain:
Butterflies of every color.
Fluttering on their way
Remind us all that Jesus lives
On this Easter day!
(*Have the butterflies dance.*)

The people who arrested Jesus didn't like him. They didn't like what Jesus did. Even though he was very kind. They didn't like what he said. Even though he taught people to love God. So they brought him to court. There they told lies about him. Then they sentenced him to die.

Refrain:
Butterflies of every color.
Fluttering on their way
Remind us all that Jesus lives
On this Easter day!
(*Have the butterflies dance.*)

They beat him and made fun of him. They called him terrible names. Then they placed him on a cross between two thieves. And they waited for him to die.

Refrain:
Butterflies of every color.
Fluttering on their way
Remind us all that Jesus lives
On this Easter day!
(*Have the butterflies dance.*)

But on the third morning, when Jesus' friends came to the garden, they got a big surprise. The stone had been rolled away. The tomb was empty. Jesus was not there. Jesus was alive!

Refrain:
Butterflies of every color.
Fluttering on their way
Remind us all that Jesus lives
On this Easter day!
(*Have the butterflies dance.*)

And in his place there sat an angel, dressed in shining white. "Do not look here for your friend. For he is not here. He is not dead. He is alive," the angel said. And Jesus' friends were amazed.

Refrain:
Butterflies of every color.
Fluttering on their way
Remind us all that Jesus lives
On this Easter day!
(*Have the butterflies dance.*)

Now we must be like Jesus friends who lived so long ago. We must tell the good news to everyone we see. Jesus is alive!

Refrain:
Butterflies of every color.
Fluttering on their way
Remind us all that Jesus lives
On this Easter day!
(*Have the butterflies dance.*)

Based on Luke 22:63-24:12.

GLUE

GLUE OR TAPE

GLUE HERE

It's Easter!
by Judy Gattis Smith

Gather the children around you. Divide the class into five groups and assign a vocal response to each group. Explain that you will be reading the Scripture, and that each group will respond each time their word is read.

Read the Response Scripture, John 20:1-4 slowly, leading the children in the appropriate responses.

Word Response
Group 1....Mary Magdalene.......”Hurray!”
Group 2......tomb...............”boo”
Group 3....run or running.......”Hurry! hurry!”
Group 4........Peter............”Ah ha”
Group 5.......disciple......... “John”

Response Scripture (John 20:1-4)

Early on the first day of the week, while it was still dark, **Mary Magdalene** *(Group 1)* came to the **tomb** *(Group 2)* and saw that the stone had been removed from the **tomb** *(Group 2)*. So she **ran** *(Group 3)* and went to **Simon Peter** *(Group 4)* and the other **disciple** *(Group 5)* the one whom Jesus loved, and **Mary** *(Group 1)* said to them: “They have taken the Lord out of the **tomb** *(Group 2)* and we do not know where they have laid him.” Then **Peter** *(Group 4)* and the other **disciple** *(Group 5)* set out and went toward the **tomb** *(Group 2)* . The two were **running** *(Group 3)* together, but the other **disciple** *(Group 5)* **out-ran** *(Group 3)* **Peter** *(Group 4)* and reached the **tomb** *(Group 2)* first.

Following the reading say: “and we know what happened next. Jesus was not there. He had risen from the dead, and the disciples' sadness was turned to joy.”

Based on John 20:1-4

Pentecost and the Early Church

God Sends a Helper

(An Echo Story)
by Mary Jane Piecrce-Norton

Have the children repeat each phrase after you and follow the actions you demonstrate.

God's people gathered to pray.
(Fold hands and bow head in prayer.)
They missed Jesus and felt afraid without him.
(Hug arms around self.)
While they prayed, they felt a great wind.
(Lift arms over head and sway side to side.)
They saw flames of fire.
(Rub hands together to look like leaping flames.)
They began to talk in many languages.
(Move hands up and down making mouth movements.)
It was very noisy.
(Clap hands and stomp feet.)
People outside heard the noise.
(Continue to clap hands and stomp feet.)
People came to see what was happening.
(Walk in place.)

When other people heard the followers of Jesus, they were amazed.
(Cup hands at ear.)
How could the followers speak in all these languages so that others could understand?
(Place hands on hips and shrug shoulders.)
Then Peter stepped forward to talk.
(Take a step in place.)
"Listen to me," he said.
(Cup hand at ear.)
"Today you can understand us because of Jesus."
(Stretch out hands in front of you.)
"Jesus helped us know God loves us."
(Point to sky.)
"This is what we were told would happen in our books of law."
(Place hands together to make an open book.)
"You can believe in Jesus and know God's love too."*(Point in front of you.)*
And many people believed.
(Place hands in front of you clasped in prayer.)

Based on Acts 2:1-16, 14, 22-28.

The Coming of the Holy Spirit

by Pam Pinkston Campbell

Make a set of red crepe paper streamers for each child. *(Make the streamers by cutting crepe paper into two or three foot strips. Join the ends of three or four strips with masking tape.)*

Say: When we come to the part of the story where we talk about the sound of a strong wind, I want you to make the sound. *(Let the children practice now.)* **Then when the story talks about tongues of flame, I want you to wave your streamers.** *(Let the children practice now.)*

How excited the disciples were to discover that Jesus, their friend and teacher, was still alive. Not only was he alive, but he was talking and eating with them, just as before.

One day Jesus called his disciples together. "Do not leave Jerusalem and return to your homes. Wait here. I must leave you, but God will send you a special helper. The spirit of God will fill each of you with great power. The spirit of God will give you strength to do the job that I have assigned you. The spirit of God will allow you to continue the job that I began. You will carry my message not just to the people of Judea, but to he very ends of the earth.

So the disciples returned to Jerusalem to wait. And while they waited, they prayed.

Soon the time came for the Feast of Weeks, a joyful time of giving thanks to God. Like Passover, many people came to Jerusalem from lands far and near to celebrate. The dis-

ciples had gathered in a house in Jerusalem to offer thanks to God for the first harvest.

Peter looked around at the group in front of him. "How we have grown," he thought to himself. "Since Jesus' death and marvelous resurrection, every day there are more and more of us. But we are still here in Jerusalem. We are still waiting—just as Jesus told us to do."

Peter thought of the people who had come to Jerusalem. Many of them had come from far away, yet many of them knew the story of Jesus. The word was indeed spreading. "Jesus promised that God would send us a special power—a helper. But it has been many days. I wonder when it will happen."

All of a sudden, a sound like the rush of a mighty wind filled the room. *(Children make wind noises.)* The people gasped. Peter looked fearfully at the other people in the room. What looked like flames danced above their heads. *(Children wave their streamers.)* Then, everyone began to talk at once.

The people inside the house made so much noise that people from the street became curious. They listened to the disciples.

"How can it be?" asked a man from another county. "These people are Galileans, yet I am able to hear what they say in my own language." Then Peter knew that the Holy Spirit had indeed come, and everyone present was filled with it.

Peter went outside the house to the crowd that had been attracted by the noise. He spoke to them, "Those of you who are worried about these people, don't be. They are filled with great joy because God's spirit has filled them. A great wind blew through the house. *(Children make wind sounds.)* And flames appeared above their heads. *(Children wave streamers.)* You remember the stories you have heard about Jesus. Jesus was truly God's Son, and what you have seen and heard is what he had promised."

"What shall we do?" the people asked.

"Repent and be baptized," said Peter. The people listened and believed. Three thousand people were baptized and became followers of Jesus that day. *(Children wave streamers.)*

The Holy Spirit was truly at work in the world, and the new church was born.

Based on Acts 2:1-43.

We Are the Church Together
by Diana Marie Bohn

As you read this story aloud, invite the children to repeat the refrain with you as they become familiar with it.

Long ago people met to worship and to pray. Though years have passed and the church has grown, we still do that today.

The church long ago was different you know, but in many ways the same.

Long ago they bowed to pray and raised their songs in praise.
Though years have passed and the church has grown, we'll worship God always.

The church long ago was different you know, but in many ways the same.

Long ago they shared together, and no one was left out.
Though years have passed and the church has grown, that's still what we're about.

The church long ago was different you know, but in many ways the same.

Long ago they spread the word that Jesus is our friend.
Though years have passed and the church has grown, his love will never end.

The church long ago was different you know, but in many ways the same.

Long ago they invited others and welcomed everyone.
Though years have passed and the church has grown, we've only just begun.

The church long ago was different you know, but in many ways the same.

Based on Acts 2:41-47.

Paul and His Friends

Paul
by Nancy Harding Groves

Have the children repeat each phrase after you and imitate the action you demonstrate.

To Damascus Paul went riding
(Pretend to hold reins, bounce.)
To find Christians who were hiding
(Wrap arms over head.)

When suddenly there shone a light
(Clap hands loudly, spreading them out, around, and down on a circle.)

Shining brighter, brighter, bright.
(Put hands in front of face, palms out, to shield eyes.)

Then Paul heard Jesus' voice
(Cup hand to ear, listening.)
And he knew he had a choice;
(Nod head yes.)

For this was Jesus' plea:
(Clasp hands as if begging.)
"Paul, Paul, why are you doing this to me?"
(Point away and then to self.)

People led him into town
(Motion forward with hands.)
He was blind, but turned around.
(Wave outstretched arms with eyes closed, feeling way.)

Once Ananias helped him see
(Lay fingers on eyes, then take away and open eyes as if surprised.)
What a Christian Paul turned out to be!
(Turn around in place.)

Based on Acts 9:1-19.

On the Road to Damascus
by LeeDell Stickler

When the children come to the expression, "For Saul was a righteous man" they will firmly pound their right fist into the outstretched palm of their left hand.

The followers of Jesus are troublemakers. We must get rid of them," said Saul, **for Saul was a righteous man.**

So Saul went from house to house in Jerusalem. Every followers of Jesus he found—every man, every woman, every child—he arrested and had them put in prison.

But this was not enough for Saul, **for Saul was a righteous man.**

"Many followers of Jesus have left the city of Jerusalem," he told the high priest. "I have heard that there are some preaching and teaching in Damascus. Let me go there and arrest them. I will bring them back to Jerusalem." And the high priest agreed, **for he too, was a righteous man.**

Saul gathered some men to go with him, and they set out for the city of Damascus. There were followers of Jesus there, and Saul intended to find them and bring them back to Jerusalem, **or Saul was a righteous man.**

As the group drew near the city, suddenly a bright light shone all around Saul. Saul fell down to the ground. From the light there came a voice: "Saul, why are you doing this?"

"Who—oo-oo is this?" Saul asked. He was afraid.

"I am Jesus, the one whose followers you are hurting. Get up, now. Go into the city. Wait and you will be told what you are to do."

Now the men who were traveling with Saul, looked around in amazement. They heard the voice. But they saw no one who could be talking to Saul.

Saul stumbled to his feet. "Help me! I can't see! Everything is dark!" he cried out.

The men took Saul by the hand and led him into Damascus. And for three days Saul sat in darkness. He was too upset to eat or drink. He waited, just as Jesus had told him, to see what was going to happen next, **for Saul was a righteous man.**

At the same time, in another part of the city, a man named Ananias also heard the voice of Jesus. "Get up and go to a certain house in the city. There you will find a man called Saul of Tarsus. Lay your hands on him so that he might see again."

"I have heard of this man," said Ananias. "He is a bad man. He has hunted down all your followers and thrown them into prison. Why should I touch him so he can see again?"

"This is the man I have chosen to bring my story to the Gentiles," said Jesus.

And Ananias did as Jesus told him. He found the house and went inside. As soon as he laid his hands on Saul, Saul's eyesight returned. For the rest of his time in Damascus, Saul told everyone, "Jesus is the Son of God." Saul, the man who once hunted down the followers of Jesus now preached the good news to all who would listen. **For Saul was a righteous man.** His life changed so much, that he even changed his name. Now, Saul would be called Paul. **For Saul was a righteous man.**

Based on Acts 9:1-21.

A Turnabout Love
by Nancy Harding Groves

Have the children repeat each phrase after you and do the motions that you demonstrate.

Have you heard of a man named Paul
(Hand to ear.)
Who turned about at Jesus' call?
(Index fingers turn around one another.)

Paul preached the faith forwhich he stood,
(Extend arm.)
And wrote great letters when he could.
(Pretend to write.)

A slave met Paul in prison in Rome,
(Pretend to grab bars.)
Far from his master Philemon's home.
(Trace house with fingers.)

Onesimus, the slave, had runaway
(Fingers running.),
Knowing punishment awaited
slaves who disobey.
(Hit open palm with fist.)

Paul taught of Jesus' love
and Onesimus found
(Cross arms over chest.)
That his life was changed,
was turned around.
(Index fingers turn around one another.)

Love caused Onesimus to turn about
(Index fingers turn around one another.),
So while in prison he helped old Paul out.
(Pretend to grab bars.)

Paul said to Onesimus, "A letter I will send,
(Pretend to write.)
And plead for your forgiveness to Philemon,
my dear friend."
(Shake hands with another child.)

Paul wrote, "I write from prison —not the
most inviting place,
(Pretend to grab bars.)
To tell you of a turnabout
and wish you peace and grace.
(Index fingers turn around one another),

" I thanked God when I heard
(Put hand to ear.)
about your love for all the saints
(Cross hands over heart.)
The story of your faith, my friend
(Shake hands with another child.),
a lovely picture paints.
(Pretend to paint.)

"And now, about your slave, Onesimus,
who ran away;
(Fingers running.)
He turned about, accepted Christ,
and serves me every day.
(Index fingers turn around one another.)

"This slave was once quite useless in the
spreading of good news,
(Shrug shoulders.)
But since he turned about you'll find he's
someone God can use.
(Index fingers turn around one another.)

"The two of you were nothing
but a master and a slave;
I send him back and hope that you'll quite
differently behave.
(Both hands push away from body.)

You know your love for Apphia (AF-ee-uh),
Archippus (ahr-KIP-uhs), and the others?
(Cross arms over chest.)
Onesimus deserves that love for now, in
Christ, you're brothers.
(Cross arms over chest.),

"If you consider us as friends
who share in ministry,
(Shake hands with another child.)
Forgive Onesimus and welcome
him as you would me.
(Use hand to beckon.)

"If this slave owes you money or has
wronged in any way,
(Pretend to count money.)
You have the word of your friend Paul:
I'll personally repay.
(Shake hands with others.)

"I know you'll do much more than
I requestwhen once you hear it.
(Put hand to ear.)
Philemon, may the grace of Jesus Christ
be with your spirit!"
(Raise arms above head.)

Paul was turned about by love
Onesimus and Philemon too;
(Index fingers turn around one another.)
That love can turn us all about
(Index fingers turn one around one another.),
including me and you!
(Point to self. Point to someone else.)

Based on Philemon.
© 1995 by Cokesbury.

God loves a cheerful giver

A Letter, A Letter
by LeeDell Stickler

Create five scrolls from a five pieces of paper and yarn. Pass the scrolls during the refrain to the beat of the poem. Begin with one scroll and as you get to each refrain, add another until all five are going. Choose Bible verses draw from Paul's letters and put simple ones on each scroll. When the chorus stops, the children who are holding letters will read the verses. Suggested verses might be: Romans 12:6, 1 Corinthians 12:13, 1 Corinthians 12:26, Ephesians 4:16, Romans 6:12, Colossians 3:2, 2 Corinthians 12:9, Ephesians 5:11, 2 Corinthians 6:17, 2 Corinthians 5:17

Refrain:
A letter, a letter,
Paul sent the churches letters.
To help them know just what to do
And follow Jesus better.

One fine day in Corinth,
Paul met a friendly pair,
Their names were Priscilla and Aquilla,
They were tentmakers there.
Together they would make their tents,
And teach and preach and pray,
When Paul moved on to Ephesus,
He told his friends to stay.

Refrain:
A letter, a letter,
Paul sent the churches letters.
To help them know just what to do
And follow Jesus better.

The Corinth church was growing
With people every day,
They came to hear about Jesus,
To worship, sing, and pray.
But members of the growing church
Soon began to fight
They wanted Paul to help them,
Decide which group was right.

Refrain:
A letter, a letter,
Paul sent the churches letters.
To help them know just what to do
And follow Jesus better.

But Paul was still in Ephesus,
A city far away,
He could not get to Corinth
But he had a lot to say.
He wrote the folks a letter,
And said, "Please get along.
We're sisters and brothers in the faith,
Don't fight about right or wrong."

Refrain:
A letter, a letter,
Paul sent the churches letters.
To help them know just what to do
And follow Jesus better.

"We're baptized with one Spirit,
In Jesus Christ you'll find
We're not Jew or Greek or slave or free,
But all of a common mind.
The gifts the Lord has given you
Are for the common good,
So work together one and all,
Just like you know you should."

Refrain:
A letter, a letter,
Paul sent the churches letters.
To help them know just what to do
And follow Jesus better.

"Love is patient, love is kind,
Neither envious nor rude.
Love provides the greatest hope,
And rejoices in the truth.
Love will never pass away,
There is no end to love.
Now faith and hope and love abide,
But the greatest of these is love.

Based on 1 Corinthians 1:10-17; 12:1-31; 13:1-12

The Gift of Love
by LeeDell Stickler

This is a good story to use for Valentine's Day. After reading the story, let the children make a "love picture" by painting a picture with hearts of different sizes and shapes. Provide heart shapes in pink, red, and white.

Reader 1: If I speak all the languages on the earth
And even speak the language of angels
And do not have love

Reader 2: Then you are a noisy gong or a clanging cymbal.

Reader 3: If I am the greatest prophet of all times and the smartest person that ever lived,
If I am filled with great faith
And do not have love.
Reader 4: Then you are nothing!

Reader 1: If I give away everything I own to the poor
And do nothing but perform good deeds for other people
And do not have love

Reader 2: Then you have gained nothing!

Reader 3: Love is patient, love is kind
Love is not envious or boastful

Reader 4: Love is not proud
Love is not rude

Reader 1: Love doesn't insist on getting its way.
Love is not grouchy or resentful.

Reader 2: Love is not happy bad things happen to people.

Reader 3: Love loves the truth.
Love hopes. Love endures.

Reader 4: Love never ends.

**All: Prophets will stop speaking.
Knowledge will come to an end
But love is forever.**

Based on 1 Corinthians 13:1-13.

Lydia
by LeeDell Stickler

Teach the children the sign language for these words: **come, pray, and God**. Use these signs to accompany the refrain.

Refrain:
Come *to the river.*
Let us sing and **pray.**
Come *to the river.*
Learn about **God** *today.*

My name is Lydia. I sell cloth—not just any cloth, but purple cloth. Purple cloth is very expensive. Only the most important people can afford to buy my cloth.

I live in the town of Philippi. It is a Roman city. The people in this city worship Roman gods. It is even against the law for people to worship any other gods. But I believe in the one true God. Every sabbath day a group of women meets by the river. We gather there to worship God and to pray because there is no synagogue in our city.

Refrain:
Come *to the river.*
Let us sing and **pray.**
Come *to the river.*
Learn about **God** *today.*

Today our group met together at the river as usual. But today a man came to join us. His name was Paul. He asked if he could join us. As we sang and prayed together, this man told us about Jesus.

Paul told us how God had come into our world through Jesus. He told us how Jesus had taught about God. He told us how Jesus had healed the sick, made the blind to see, and even raised the dead. He told us of all the wonderful things that Jesus had done.

Refrain:
Come *to the river.*
Let us sing and **pray.**
Come *to the river.*
Learn about **God** *today.*

Then Paul told us how Jesus had been arrested and put to death. He told us how God had raised Jesus from the dead. Then Paul told us how he had met Jesus on the road to Damascus. Paul told us how Jesus had changed his life forever.

The more Paul talked about this man Jesus, the more I knew that I wanted to be a follower of Jesus too.

"I want to be a follower of Jesus. Come to my house. Tell the story of Jesus to everyone there," I told Paul. "Baptize me and my whole household." And that is just what Paul did.

Based on Acts 16:6-15.

Sunday School, the Bible, and Other Things

Praise God
by Daphna Flegal

This is a good activity to "get the wiggles out" of a group of children who need to move from a more active activity to a quieter one.

Clap, clap, clap your praise,
(Clap hands.)
Clap your praise to God.
Praise God!

Shake, shake, shake your praise,
(Shake hands.)
Shake your praise to God.
Praise God!
Shout, shout, shout your praise,
(Cup hands around mouth and speak loudly.)
Shout your praise to God.
Praise God!

Whisper, whisper, whisper your praise,
(Put first finger to lips and whisper this verse.)
Whisper your praise to God.
Praise God!

Based on Psalm 95.

Everyone Has A Part

by Susan Isbell

Hands that help
(Extend hands open, palms up.)
Hearts that care
(Clasp both hands over heart.)
The Bible says;
(Hold hands in front of you like an open book.)
It's good to share.
(Join your two hands in front.)
A helping hand,
(Extend one hand.)
A caring heart,
(Clasp hands over heart.)
Each of us,
(Point to each other.)
Can do our part.
(Continue pointing.)
A voice to tell,
(Touch lips with finger.)
A story to teach,
(Hold hands in front like an open book.)
Some can pray,
(Hands praying.)
Others can preach.
(Cup hands around mouth.)
I can help,
(Point to self.)
And so can you,
(Point to someone else.)
Each of us,
(Point to several others.)
Has a job to do!
(Continue pointing.)

A Prayer of Thanks

by LeeDell Stickler

Have the children do the actions with each verse of the prayer. On the response, the children are to fold their hands in front as if praying.

Response: *Amen, I say, Amen.*

I thank you, God, that at the start,
You made the sky and sea.
(Point with index finger and make a bow shape across the sky. Use the same hand to indicate wave motions for water.)
I thank you, God, for all the things
You put there just for me.
(Point to self.)

Response: *Amen, I say, Amen.*

I thank you, God, for earth and sky,
For grass and wind and trees.
(Pretend to be a tree.)
For birds and fish and animals,
I thank you, God, for these.
(Line thumbs and flap hands as bird, make bunny rabbit with right hand and hop across the body.)

Response: *Amen, I say, Amen.*

I thank you, God, for snow and rain
And rainbows in the sky.
(Hold hands up and wiggle fingers as you bring the hands down to indicate rain.)
I thank you, God, for sunny days
Where clouds go rushing by.
(Hold hands above head and move from left to right as if clouds moving by.)

Response: *Amen, I say, Amen.*

And most of all, I thank you, God,
For those who help me grow.
(Squat down and become small then stand up very tall.)
And learn to follow Jesus,
The greatest gift I know.
(Cross arms over chest.)

Response: *Amen, I say, Amen.*

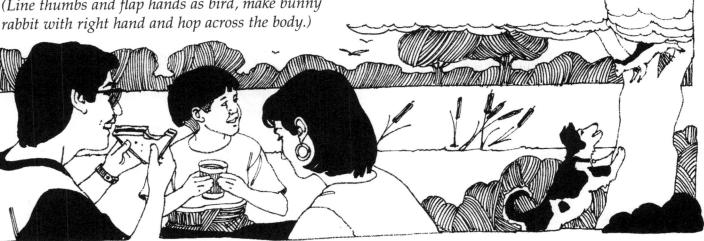

The Bible
by LeeDell Stickler

Create small picture cards prior to the time together. Pass out the cards. Have the children listen carefully for their word/picture. When they hear it they stand up and hold the card up. Words in bold are suggested words. If you have more children, identify more words. If you have fewer children, use only those for that number.

The **Bible** is a treasure **book**
This I truly know
It tells about God's **people**
Who lived so long ago.
It tells about creation
How darkness turned to light.
It tells about the **sun** and **moon**
And **stars** that fill the night.
It tells about the earth and seas
And how the world began.
How God created animals
And plants and woman and man.

The Bible is a treasure book
Of this there is no doubt.
It tells about God's people
When **Moses** led them out.
It tells about the Exodus
And how they crossed the **sea**
Walking on the sandy path
God made God's people free.
It tells about God's people
Who learned to be faithful and true
How God's Commandments taught them
To live as God wanted them to.

The Bible tells about Jesus
And the **stable** where he was born.
It tells about the **fishermen**
That Jesus called that morn.
The Bible tells about God's great **love**
In every single page.
The stories have been passed to me
From some far distant age.
With every story that I learn
It's message lives in me.
And I can share God's treasure book
With everyone I see.

Wonderful Book of God's People

by New Invitation Team

Make two signs on construction paper.
Sign #1: Shout the name of a Bible person you know.
Sign #2: Shout your name.

Say: I want you to join me in an echo litany. In this litany, you will repeat everything I say, just the way I say it. When I get to a certain point in the litany, I am going to hold up a sign. Read the sign and follow the directions.

onderful
(Whisper.)

Wonderful Wonderful Wonderful Wonderful
(Use a fast whisper.)

Wooonderful
(Use a soft voice; draw it out.)

Book!
(Use a normal voice, but with a clipped pronunciation.)

A book, a book, a book, a book
(Increase volume each time.)

a Wonderful Book!
*(Use a normal voice in volume
but an excited tone.)*

People. *(Use normal voice.)*

GOD'S people
(Emphasize God.)

Who's people?
(Raise voice on last word.)

God's people!
(Say emphatically.)

Wonderful book
(Whisper.)

God's people
(Loud.)
(Show sign that says: Shout the name of someone from the Bible.)

Wonderful book
(Say it loudly.)

God's people
(Whisper.)
(Show sign that says: Shout your name.)

Wonderful Book of God's People!
(Whisper.)

Wonderful Book of God's People
(Speak louder.)

Wonderful Book of God's People!
(Shout!)

ndex of Bible References

ndex of Titles